THE FIFTH QUARTER

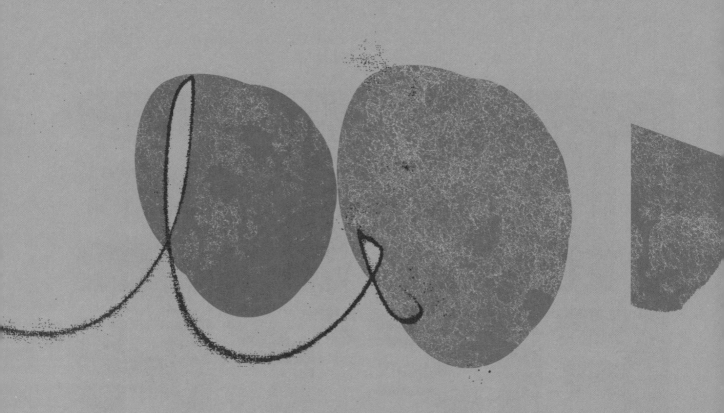

FOR ANNE-MARIE AND GUY

THE FIFTH QUARTER

ANISSA HELOU

First published in Great Britain in 2004 by
Absolute Press
Scarborough House
29 James Street West
Bath BA1 2BT
Phone 44 (0) 1225 316013
Fax 44 (0) 1225 445836
E-mail info@absolutepress.co.uk
Website www.absolutepress.co.uk

Publisher Jon Croft
Commissioning Editor Meg Avent
Designer Matt Inwood

Illustrations Andy Pedler

A catalogue record of this book is available from the
British Library

ISBN 1 904573 21 5

Printed and bound by Lego, Italy

CONTENTS

FOREWORD

I love eating offal, but it has not always been so. Throughout my childhood and early youth I shared the predominant modern Anglo Saxon squeamishness about eating the 'organs and edges' of our meat animals. It's hard to say where this squeamishness comes from. Childish reactions (in every sense) to these foods seem almost inbuilt in our culture, so that school age kids are saying 'liver, yuk!' and 'Eurgghh! Not tongue' before they have the least idea what either meat tastes like.

But of course this is misleading. Offer a toddler, still uncorrupted in taste by his or her peers, a piece of liver with encouragement and the chances are he or she will devour it with enthusiasm. The learned revulsion is an adult prejudice passed to children unintentionally – but without much regret either.

It's hard to understand the precise origins of such a sweeping generalisation of the national culinary attitude. But it certainly has to do with the post-war industrialisation of farming in general, and of meat production in particular. As the prime cuts of muscle meat became cheaper and cheaper, an increasingly affluent society felt the provision of lean red meat was a symbol of (relative) comfort. And the regular provision of lean red meat – particularly in the archetypal Sunday roast – became a matter of family pride.

The conspicuous rejection of offal was another way to make the same point – as if to say 'we don't need to eat that cheap stuff anymore'. It was undoubtedly re-inforced by a kind of post-war food jingoism too, whereby offal became a potent example of exotic food, dismissed with such arrogant philistinism as 'that foreign muck'. It's ironic that we are now falling over ourselves to praise and feast on exotic foreign dishes – yet we are still showing a marked reluctance to engage with offal.

More encouragingly, I have often noticed that the pre-war generation retain an affection for the offal – particularly tripe, brains, hearts and trotters – that their children so resolutely refuse. And I also see signs that a younger generation are proving more adventurous than their parents. When I recently took a dish of tripe to the local farmers market, it was notably the over-seventies, and the under-thirties, who were most enthusiastic. The young are now enjoying a far more broad-minded culinary cultural inheritance, and that can surely include rediscovering the pleasures of offal.

My own conversion came while working as a sous-chef at the River Café in London. My boss Rose Gray pointed out the absurdity of a young man who professed a passion for food and an adventurous palate turning away from a whole raft of exciting tastes and textures. She quickly weaned me on the finest calves' liver, and I soon graduated to an appreciation of kidneys, tongues, sweetbreads and – now one of my favourite treats – brains.

Since then I have been evangelical in my enthusiasm for offal. I want as many people as possible to appreciate that the 'Fifth Quarter' offers us some of the most distinctive, and some of the most subtle, tastes and textures that we can find in the vast food firmament. And I want them to realize that overcoming a food aversion, and learning truly to relish and appreciate a food that you once disliked or dismissed, is not only a satisfying triumph in the kitchen. It's a little victory in life, as well.

And so I am delighted that a contemporary food writer has taken on the bold and adventurous task of writing a whole book about offal – and I am particularly delighted that that writer is Anissa Helou.

Anissa understands that a holistic approach to butchery and cookery is the only one that does right by the animals we raise and kill for food. That we owe it to them not only to show them respect and good husbandry while they are alive, but also to make the best use of every last part of them once they are dead.

But she also understands that it is not through preaching about principal that we will convert more cooks and diners to the joys of offal. It is by offering them a selection of exciting and delightful recipes, from the global gamut of food cultures, that demonstrate the sheer versatility of offal, and the immense pleasure to be had by exploring these foods. That is what she has done and I salute her for it.

Hugh Fearnley-Whittingstall
October 2004

INTRODUCTION

'The 'inwards' are next taken out, and if the wife be not a slattern, here, in the mere offal, in the mere garbage, there is food, and delicate food too, for a large family for a week; and hog's puddings for the children, and some for neighbours' children, who come to play with them; for these things are by no means to be overlooked, seeing that they tend to the keeping alive of that affection in children for their parents, which later in life will be found absolutely necessary to give effect to wholesome precept, especially when opposed to the boisterous passions of youth.'
Cottage Economy, William Cobbett, London 1821

The 'Fifth Quarter', or 'il Quinto Quarto' as it is known in Italy, is, of course, a contradiction in terms. There is no such thing as a fifth quarter. Yet, this seemingly absurd term is the one used by both French and Italian butchers to describe those parts of the animal – head, tail, feet and innards – that do not belong to the four quarters of the carcass.

In England the term used is rather more prosaic and off-putting. The extremities and innards are known baldly as 'offal' – that which falls, or is thrown off (as defined by the OED) – while in America the description is completely non-descript, as it were: 'organ' or 'variety meats'. And this, in a way, illustrates the current anglo-saxon attitude towards offal. Most English and American people have no taste for or have lost their appreciation of it, while the French, Latins, Asians, Scandinavians and Africans are still keen on both the taste and the texture.

I belong to the Asian group, born and brought up in the Lebanon, on the eastern shores of the Mediterranean. And from the moment when I was able to chew properly, I ate raw liver for breakfast, stuffed tripe and intestines for lunch and fried testicles for dinner. And during the 21 years that I lived in Beirut, I could, whenever I wanted to and provided I woke up early enough, go and watch our local butcher slaughter his animals, gut them and hang the washed pieces high.

Skinned sheep's heads looked amazingly and scarily alive, their bared teeth fixed into a leering grin, the mouth just open enough to let the tongue hang out at the side as if mocking the passers-by. Intestines were pumped full of air and curled surprisingly attractively in buckets, while feet were stacked neatly and cleanly on marble counters. Stomachs were spiked through meat hooks and hung in pouches alongside the heart, lungs and liver. Testicles were left attached to the halved carcasses to indicate the gender.

Lamb's offal was not the only offal we sought or were offered. Our chickens came complete with head and feet still on, and the giblets inside. Whenever my mother boiled one, my siblings and I would argue about whose turn it was to have the head or the feet. My mother had taught us how to crack open the chicken's skull to remove the tiny brains without damaging them; and she had also shown us how to peel the lizard-like skin off the feet to enjoy the gelatinous meat.

We also loved and feasted on fish heads and brains. With these, there was no tussle as to who would get the head. Most of the time, my mother cooked small enough fish for each us to have our own.

But my favourite memory of eating offal in the Lebanon is that of the wonderful raw liver that we as a family would enjoy for breakfast – one of the greatest of all delicacies. The liver still warm, straight from the recently slaughtered animal, tasting unbelievably fresh. Cut into small pieces, we would place one or two bits of liver on pitta bread, add a cube of fat from the tail, season with sea salt and 7-spice mixture, and then tuck in. The texture, taste and temperature of the meat were perfect; more blood than room temperature, with a real taste of meat without any gamey undertones, and with a smooth, silky texture. It was pure bliss.

There are many reasons why the Lebanese and many other cultures prize the 'fifth quarter' so highly. Firstly, for its sheer rarity value. There is simply a lot less offal than meat on an animal, and the few bits there are, are considered choice morsels. Just think how many kilograms of meat there are on a calf's carcass and how little offal there is in comparison: a brain weighing a few hundred grams, a liver weighing 3-4 kilograms or so, and less than 1 kilogram in sweetbreads. Tripe is probably the only part of the 'fifth quarter' which has significant volume, but even that is still minimal in relation to the volume of meat.

And then there is the sheer culinary and gastronomic delight in eating offal. The texture, delicate in some parts, chewy or simply unusual in others, makes offal all the more highly prized. When cooked properly, brains will melt in the mouth, kidneys will be chewy without being tough, and ears will have an addictive crunch. The variety of sensual pleasures is seemingly endless and so much more varied than plain meat eating.

Quite apart from the rarity value and the sensual pleasures to be gained from living a life that includes offal, there is also the simple fact that it seems wrong and wasteful to discard any edible part of an animal. There is something undeniably satisfying in knowing that all the parts of an animal are used and enjoyed.

And the final reason why offal should begin to be taken more seriously again is for its simple nutritional value. Most offal is low in fat and high in protein and is an excellent source of vitamins and minerals.

In writing this book I hope to encourage my readers to experiment wholeheartedly with the 'fifth quarter'. I have chosen a limited, albeit wide-ranging, collection of international recipes that includes some classics and some personal favourites. A truly comprehensive selection would have needed several volumes. Some of the recipes are simple and quick to make while others are more complex and require more time. But whatever and however you choose to cook, I hope that you will begin to appreciate the many culinary and gastronomic joys of the much neglected world of 'The Fifth Quarter'.

Anissa Helou
London, July 2004

THE ACCEPTABLE FACE OF OFFAL

At the first mention of offal, most people will think what, tripe? Hate it. It will not occur to them that if they hate offal, they should also hate caviar, foie gras or chicken wings. Yet, all are indeed innards and extremities but belong to what I call 'the acceptable face of offal'.

Caviar is the salted eggs of different species of sturgeon: sevruga, beluga and oscietre. The very rare 'golden' caviar is nothing more than oscietre from albino fish and, even though the price is tremendous, more than double that of the best caviar, many wonder if it is worth it.

The notion of caviar as a luxury food is not modern. It was mentioned by Rabelais, back in the 16th century, as the finest item from what would now be called hors d'oeuvre; and there is a reference to 'the caviar of the general' in Shakespeare. However, it wasn't until the 19th century that caviar acquired the widespread cachet it has today.

The best way to serve caviar is plain, with toast or blinis and sour cream or unsalted butter. Caviar is also wonderful in soft-boiled eggs or jacket potatoes with crème fraîche. The tin should be opened just before serving and, in the unlikely event there are any left-overs, these should be consumed within 24 hours. The spoons used to serve or eat caviar should be non-metallic, ideally horn or mother of pearl.

Salmon roe is poor man's caviar, costing a fraction of the price. Still, it is delicious and I love the way the big, juicy eggs pop open as you bite them. Salmon roe is used in sushi or, as with its more elevated cousin, served on blinis.

Other highly prized fish eggs are those of the humble grey mullet. The roe is taken out intact in its membrane and is then salted, pressed and dried in the sun, after which it is sealed in wax or vacuum-packed. The cured roe is known as bottarga in Italian, boutargue or poutargue in French and batrakh in Arabic. It is found in most Mediterranean countries. In Greece, it is eaten thinly sliced or made into taramosalata, though most taramosalata nowadays is made with the much cheaper **cod's roe**. Cod's roe can also be eaten fresh when it is in season – from the end of January to the beginning of March – boiled in salt water for 4 hours, then simply sliced and sautéed in butter. In Italy, bottarga, which can also be tuna's, is shaved or grated over pasta, and in lebanon it is very much part of the mezze menu, served thinly sliced, topped with sliced garlic and drizzled with olive oil.

And then there is **herring roe**, where in England it is sold fresh and fried in butter to serve on toast, while in Japan, it is salted or pickled. Herring roe represents fertility in Japan and is a typical traditional new year's dish there. The hard roe is that of female fish, while the soft roe, also called white roe, is the milt or reproductive glands of male fish.

Another very acceptable offal is **foie gras**, a delicacy dating back to the times of the Greeks and Romans. The Jews are credited with introducing the method of force-feeding ducks and geese for foie gras into Europe. The way to fatten ducks is slightly different from that for geese. Ducks are fed twice a day for about 2 weeks while geese are fed three to four times a day for almost a month. The liver expands to 6-10 times its normal size. Even though the method is pretty cruel – a funnel is inserted into the bird's mouth and feed is crammed into it – the resulting foie gras is so exquisite that most people, myself included, put aside their social conscience when it comes to eating it. There are three basic ways of preparing foie gras. All are very simple. You can cover it in salt and let the salt 'cook' it, bake it in the oven in a terrine or 'en papillotes', or sauté it in a pan. You can also make mousse de foie gras, but this seems to me a waste, unless you have broken-up left overs.

Bone marrow is another simple and acceptable offal delicacy. The marrow is in the shin bones of oxes or calves and can either be poached or roasted in its bone, or alternatively the bone can be broken up to release the marrow which can then be poached and served on toast or steak. According to Dorothy Hartley, author of the classic *Food in England*, bone marrow was used mostly in sweet dishes in the middle ages, but by the time Queen Victoria came to reign, bone marrow had become a man's food and was considered 'unladylike'.

Chicken wings are certainly not considered a delicacy but they are, nevertheless, a very acceptable face of offal. Wings may not form part of the giblets here or in America, but in France, the tip and middle part belong to the abatis (or abattis, the french word for poultry offal). The tips are discarded or used in broths and the middle parts are generally marinated and barbecued or roasted in the oven. The marinade varies according to the country. In Lebanon, for example, it is garlicky and spicy, while in America it is sweet and sour.

And finally, there are two last contenders for the acceptable face of offal which are possibly the most acceptable of all: **sausages and pâtés** which people eat without even realising they are eating offal. Of course, not all pâtés have offal in them but in the case of sausages, all do, if only for the casing which, unless it is synthetic, is inevitably intestines.

All this is to say that if you have been reckless enough to enjoy offal without realising it, why not put aside your prejudices and squeamishness and try some of the more extreme bits. You may not want to go so far as eating raw liver for breakfast, as I did when young in the Lebanon, but perhaps you may want to try sautéed sweetbreads or testicles. And who knows, you may never look back to your pre-offal days and eventually graduate to eating that ultimate test of offal accomplishment, sheep's eyes. You will then discover that they are not only delicious, but also very close in texture to a perfectly acceptable fish, squid!

FOIE GRAS AU SEL

FOIE GRAS EN PAPILLOTE

This is my favourite way of preparing foie gras. By cooking the livers in salt, there is hardly any loss. It was my great friend, Anne-Marie de Rougemont to whom this book is dedicated, who first taught me how to prepare foie gras this way. She herself was given the recipe by Jean-Paul Boy, currently the owner of two of the best restaurants in Nîmes, le Tango and Neuf. I prefer to use ducks' liver rather than goose, as they are smaller and somewhat less fatty.

Here is what you need to do with 1 duck's liver weighing about 600g. First remove as much of the nerves as you can. Open up the lobes and slide a knife under the nerves to losen them before pulling – be sure not to destroy the liver in the process. Once you have discarded the nerves, place the liver in a bowl, season it with sea salt and pepper to taste and marinate it for 12 hours using a 50-50 mixture of white wine and Tio Pepe sherry – the liquid must cover the liver.

When the time is up, remove the liver from the marinade and roll it tightly in a cheese cloth. Spread a thick layer of coarse sea salt on a platter and place the wrapped liver on the salt. Cover completely with sea salt, making sure that the sides are also covered, and leave for 12 hours in the refrigerator. Do not leave any longer than 12 hours or the liver will become too salty.

Make an aspic with the marinade following the instructions on the gelatine packet. Once the aspic has set, cut it into small cubes. Unwrap the liver and place on a serving platter. Surround with the aspic cubes. Serve chilled with a Sauternes, either as a starter for 10-12 or a as a main course for 6.

This is a particularly wonderful and extremely simple way of preparing foie gras.

Cut the liver into 2-3cm thick slices, removing the nerves as you find them. Lay each slice on a large piece of foil. Season with salt and pepper to taste. Wrap the foil very loosely around the liver, leaving quite a bit of space at the top – be sure to seal the foil well or else the fat will run out. Bake in a very hot oven for 7-8 minutes. Serve immediately with a warm green bean salad dressed with the vinaigrette on page 128.

FOIE GRAS ESCALOPES WITH STEWED BABY ONIONS

ESCALOPES DE FOIE GRAS AUX PETIT OIGONS CONFITS

I still remember the occasion, even though it happened more than twenty years ago. A wealthy Kuwaiti friend had invited a group of us to the newest, best and most talked about restaurant in town, Nico's in Queenstown Road. Clapham was still the back of beyond then and none of us was that keen on driving south of the river, however good the restaurant. But she insisted, and so we all trekked to Queenstown Road, feeling as if we were embarking on a real adventure. Of course, the meal was a sensation! Nico Ladenis eventually acquired three Michelin stars, Clapham become trendy and London has since become awash with excellent restaurants. This recipe from Nico's days in Queenstown Road is a perfect example of his great talent.

24 really small baby onions, peeled and trimmed
1 fresh goose liver
Unsalted butter
Sea salt and freshly ground black pepper
Chives for garnish

For the sauce
Red wine
Veal stock
Cognac

Blanch the baby onions.

Slice the goose liver into 4 long, thin slices. Season with salt and pepper and fry quickly, ideally in a dry copper frying pan, leaving the liver quite pink inside. Keep the onions and liver warm while you prepare the sauce.

Pour the fat out of the pan – reserve to sauté potatoes or other vegetables. Deglaze the pan with a little red wine. Boil until almost completely evaporated then add some veal stock. Reduce and add a little cognac. Taste and adjust the seasoning if necessary.

Place each escalope on a warmed plate. Scatter six onions around each and carefully cover with a quarter of the sauce. Garnish with chives and serve immediately.

SERVES 4

JENNIFER PATTERSON'S HERRING ROE ON TOAST

I found this supremely comforting recipe in Arabella Boxer's *Book of English Food*. Savouries in England were, and occasionally still are, served with high tea or after pudding, but I prefer to have these roe either for breakfast or as a starter.

8 medium soft herring roes
2 thin rashers unsmoked streaky bacon
2 large slices fairly thick brown or white bread, toasted
1 teaspoon anchovy paste, or Gentleman's Relish
30g plain flour
30g unsalted butter
1 tablespoon sunflower oil
Sea salt and cayenne pepper
1 tablespoon finely chopped flat-leaf parsley
Lemon wedges

Wash the roes under cold water to remove the slime and stiffen them. Dry with kitchen paper, then dip in the flour to coat all over. Shake off the excess flour.

Grill the bacon under a pre-heated grill until completely crisp. Remove onto kitchen paper to drain off any excess fat.

While the roe is cooking, make the toast and spread it with the anchovy paste or Gentleman's Relish.

Melt the butter in a large frying pan over medium heat. Add the oil and when it is just sizzling, add the roes and cook until golden, about 3-4 minutes on each side. Remove to drain on kitchen paper.

Pile equal quantities of roe on the toasts. Season with salt to taste and a little cayenne pepper. Crumble equal quantities of bacon over each and sprinkle the parsley all over. Serve immediately with the lemon wedges.

SERVES 2

COD'S ROE DIP

TARAMOSALATA

Making taramosalata is so simple and the home-made results so superior to shop-bought that I really don't understand why it isn't a staple for all domestic cooks. You can make a really fancy taramosalata by using roe from grey mullet (bottarga), or alternatively a more common but equally delicious and cheaper one by using cod's roe.

350g smoked cod's roe (or bottarga)
Juice of 1½-2 lemons
250ml extra virgin olive oil

Put the roe in the food processor with the lemon juice. Process until completely pulverised.

Slowly add the oil until you have a mixture which is the consistency of a rather soft potato purée. Three quarters of the way through adding the oil, taste for tartness and add more lemon juice if the mixture is too bland. Serve with very good bread.

SERVES 4-6

ROASTED BONE MARROW

Dorothy Hartley, author of the classic *Food in England*, says of marrow that it is 'the most light and digestible of fats, and should be given to children and invalids who require building up'. Well, whatever its nutritional value, one thing is certain, it is one of the most delicious and accessible of offal dishes and has long been favoured by the English domestic cook. Indeed, in medieval times it was often used in sweet preparations. While in Georgian times they would bake the marrow bones, covering the cut end with a small crust to stop evaporation; the baked bones would then be wrapped in white napkins and served with a special long silver marrow-spoon, which was used to scoop out the delectable marrow. Bones were also boiled, standing on their knuckle end, leaving the top, cut end out of the water. The cooked marrow was then scooped out and either eaten off the spoon or spread on toast, seasoned with salt and pepper.

Baking marrow bones takes about 20 minutes in a hot oven, while boiling them will take approximately 1 hour. It is always a good idea to test for doneness by inserting a thin knife into the marrow. Once the marrow is done, serve with sea salt and pepper and wafer-thin toast, as they did in Georgian times, or with thick slices of toasted sourdough as they do at St John's restaurant in Clerkenwell in London.

You can also take the marrow out of the bone and blanch it. Ask your butcher to give you thick marrow bones in sections of about 5cm long, and ask him to split the bones in several places so that it is easy for you to crack them open to release the pieces of marrow. Blanch the marrow for 5 minutes. Test with a knife to see if it is done and immediately serve on toast or on rare steak with sea salt and pepper.

BONE MARROW PATTIES

BONE MARROW BUTTER

The following delightful recipe comes from Ambrose Heath's *Meat* book and is transcribed verbatim.

Beef marrow bones
Cold water
Puff pastry
Parsley
Chives
Thyme
1 tablespoon cream
Salt and pepper
Lemon juice

Have the bones broken so that the marrow can be got out in walnut-sized pieces, and put these into a pan with a pinch of salt and cover them with cold water. Then boil for a minute or two, and pass through a nylon or hair sieve. Have ready 6 pattypans lined with puff pastry and beat 1 tablespoonful cream with a finely minced tablespoonful of parsley, chives and thyme mixed together. Season with lemon juice, salt and pepper and put a little of this with the pieces of marrow in the pattypans. Bake in a moderate oven for 15 minutes and serve at once.

SERVES 6

This is probably the ultimate recipe in the canon of the acceptable face of offal, as no one will even know they are eating offal unless, of course, you tell them. Not only that but, according to Dorothy Hartley, it 'is excellent for thin nervous children'. So, if you have them, get to work and use the marrow butter in their sandwiches instead of regular butter. They won't be any the wiser and, who knows, Hartley may well turn out to be right.

3-5kg marrow bones
Pinch sugar
Good pinch saffron threads, powdered

Break the bones with a cleaver or ask you butcher to do it for you. Place the bones in a very clean roasting dish and put in a cool oven, about 110-130°C/225-250°F/ Gas ¼-½. Leave until all the marrow has melted out of the bones.

Strain the fat through a cheese cloth or a hair sieve and collect in a mixing bowl. Add the sugar and saffron and whisk like whipped cream. This will make the marrow butter very light, but you can also let it set as is. In either case use it as you would butter.

YIELDS 300-500g

GRILLED CHICKEN WINGS

JAWANEH DJAJ

The following method for preparing chicken wings, especially when grilled over a charcoal fire, is famously moreish – a whole platter has been known to disappear in minutes. So I have catered for this by giving a recipe for large quantities. You can use the marinade for other meats, such as chicken livers or even plain lamb or chicken.

12 large garlic cloves, peeled and crushed
4 tablespoons extra virgin olive oil
Juice of 2 lemons, or to taste
1/4 teaspoon ground cinnamon
1 teaspoon Lebanese seven-spice mixture
    (or ground allspice)
1/2 teaspoon finely ground black pepper
Good pinch cayenne pepper (optional)
Sea salt to taste
24 medium organic chicken wings, rinsed and
    patted dry

Put the crushed garlic in a large mixing bowl.
Add the olive oil, lemon juice and seasonings and mix well. Add the chicken wings and stir to coat evenly with the marinade. Let marinate in a cool place for at least 1 hour, stirring occasionally.

Arrange the chicken wings on a rack and place under a pre-heated grill or over a barbecue fire. Cook for about 5-7 minutes on each side or until golden brown all over and slightly charred in places and completely done. Serve hot with the garlic dip on page 122.

SERVES 4-6

TERRINE OF GAME

A simple and quick recipe for a classic game terrine.

450g mixed game meat
225g veal
225g calf's liver
225 calf's kidney
1 teaspoon ground allspice
1 teaspoon ground coriander
2 cloves garlic
2 teaspoons sea salt
Freshly ground black pepper
Zest of 1 orange
Juice of 1 orange
125g breadcrumbs
1 small glass of Curacao
Pistachio nuts
A little unsalted butter to grease the terrine
Streaky bacon to line the terrine

Put all the ingredients, except for the bacon and nuts, in a food processor. Process until the mixture is very finely chopped. Transfer to a mixing bowl and add the pistachio nuts to taste.

Grease a rectangular terrine with a little butter and line with the streaky bacon. Spoon the meat mixture into the lined terrine and bake in a bain-marie in a warm oven at 180 C for about 45 minutes.

Remove from the oven, place a weight over the terrine and let cool. Leave it to rest in the refrigerator for 24 hours before serving slightly chilled, perhaps accompanied with a Cumberland sauce.

SERVES 12

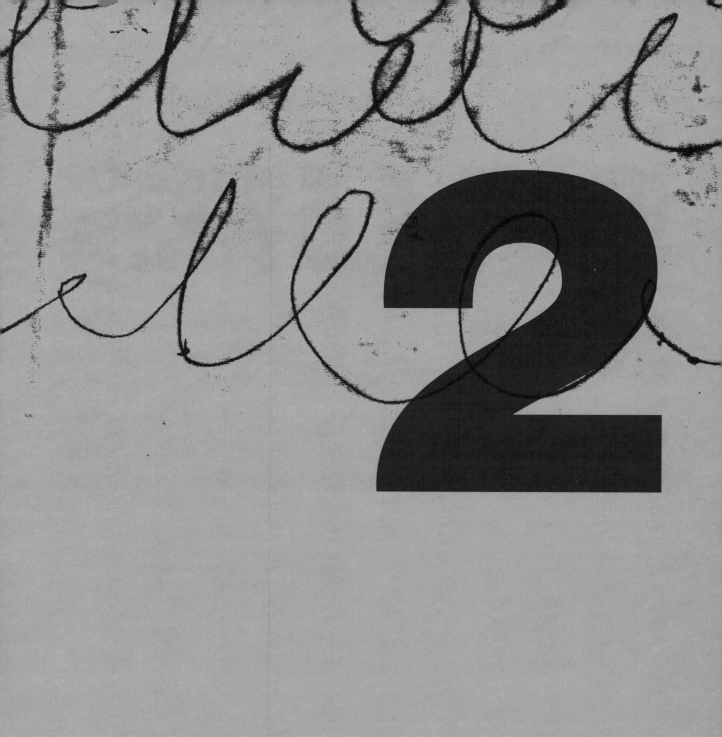

2

SOUPS
SALADS &
STARTERS

TURKISH TRIPE SOUP

ISKEMBE ÇORBASI

In the western Mediterranean tripe is sold already cleaned and cooked. In Middle Eastern countries, however, tripe is sold uncooked, although most of the time it will have already been cleaned. Not cleaned enough though to spare you the chore of having to wash it in several changes of soap and water.
Here, in the UK, ox tripe is sold mostly bleached.
A shame really, as most of the texture and taste goes in the process. In Turkey, tripe soup is a breakfast speciality, sold in specialist restaurants and cafés.
A similar version is also popular in Greece (patsas) and, again, it is consumed early in the morning, often after a night's drinking.

300g piece of uncooked sheep's tripe
Sea salt
75g unsalted butter
1½ tablespoons all-purpose flour
2 egg yolks
juice of half a lemon, or to taste
¼ teaspoon cayenne
¼ teaspoon paprika
6 garlic cloves, crushed, mixed with 125ml vinegar
  (White wine or Champagne)

Wash the tripe in several changes of soap and water and rinse well. Put in a large saucepan and add 1½ litres of water. Place over a medium-high heat, add salt to taste and bring to the boil. As the water comes to the boil, skim the surface clean and cover the pan. Lower the heat and simmer for 1½ hours or until tender.

When the tripe is done, remove and slice into thin strips. Strain the stock and set aside.

Melt 3 tablespoons of butter in a clean saucepan and stir in the flour. Slowly add the strained tripe stock while continuing to stir. Add the tripe and simmer for 5 minutes.

Beat the eggs together with the lemon juice.

Melt the rest of the butter in a frying pan. Stir in the cayenne and paprika. Set aside.

Add a little of the hot soup liquid to the egg mixture and then pour the egg mixture into the soup stirring all the time. Remove from the heat and stir in the garlic and vinegar. (Usually the garlic-vinegar mixture is served on the side for people to help themselves but I prefer to mix it all in.)

Taste and adjust the seasoning of the soup. Then pour into a pre-heated tureen and drizzle the flavoured butter all over. Serve very hot with good bread.

SERVES 6

YOUGOSLAV SPICY SOUP

JAGNJEĆA SARMA

This Yougoslav recipe is traditionally served with kajmak, a kind of very thick, white clotted cream.

1 lamb's liver
A pair of lamb's lungs
1 lamb's heart
Sea salt and freshly ground black pepper
4 tablespoons extra virgin olive oil
1-2 tablespoons flour
Paprika
Milk
Kajmak (or crème fraîche)
Parsley

Rinse and drain the liver, lungs and heart and put them in a large saucepan. Cover with water and bring to the boil. Drain and discard the water. Dice the meats into 5cm square cubes and return to the saucepan. Barely cover with water, add salt and pepper to taste and bring to the boil over a medium high heat, then lower the heat and simmer for 1 hour.

Just before the meat is done, heat the oil in a small frying pan. Fry the flour for a couple of minutes, stirring continuously. Stir in the paprika and then slowly add the mixture to the soup, stirring all the while. Continue stirring for about 5 minutes or until the soup has thickened.

Add enough milk to the soup to achieve a nice milky consistency. Serve very hot with the kajmak and chopped parsley. Just drop a spoonful of kajmak (or crème fraîche) into each serving of the soup and garnish with chopped parsley.

SERVES 6-8

MUSLIM OXTAIL SOUP

SUP HANG WUA

I have adapted the following recipe from David Thompson's magisterial Thai Food. It is very simple to make, especially if you decide to use commercial curry powder. Ginger water is made by soaking bruised ginger and a little sugar in water for about 10 minutes; the water is then strained and used in recipes that call for it, as below.

3kg oxtail, cut into segments and blanched
5 onions, chopped
5 cups ginger water
4 heaped tablespoons curry powder
Sea salt
Pinch ground white pepper
A few bird's eye chillies, to taste
1 tablespoon chopped coriander leaves
3 tablespoons deep-fried shallots, preferably cooked in ghee
Lime wedges

Rinse the oxtail and place in a saucepan with the onion and ginger water. Add the curry powder, a little salt to taste, the white pepper and cover the meat with water. Bring to the boil. Then simmer for about 3-4 hours or until the meat is tender and the onions completely dissolved. Skim every now and then during cooking.

Serve the soup seasoned with chillies, coriander and the deep-fried shallots, with the lime wedges on the side. The soup should taste aromatic and rich.

SERVES 4-6

FISH TRIPE SOUP

KAPOH PLA

My great friend, Vippy Rangsit, who lives in Thailand, employs probably the best Thai cook, Tiew, that I have ever met. And it was Tiew who provided me with this recipe. The fish tripe doesn't have much flavour but the texture is soft and gelatinous and rather sexy. The taste is slightly sour and the soup is thick with the tripe, mushrooms, shredded chicken, vegetables and quail eggs. Some people also add cubes of pig's blood at the end. The soup is a popular light meal, ideal for when people want more than a snack but less than a full meal. They eat it mostly in the evening when they are rushing around, or late at night when it is too late to eat something more substantial.

Soak 10 pieces of fish stomach (about 100g) for 30 minutes. Then put the tripe in boiling water with 2 or 3 chunks of fresh ginger – this is done to absorb the fishy smell. Boil for 10 minutes. Drain, squeeze out as much water as you can and transfer to a bowl. There is no need to refrigerate the fish tripe.

While the tripe is soaking, make a dense chicken broth using a whole chicken, garlic, coriander roots, ginger and soy sauce. Start with about 1.5 litres water, which you will then boil down to 750ml. Strain the broth into a clean saucepan and reserve the chicken.

Soak a good-sized handful of dried shitakes in warm water for an hour. (If you use whole dry shitakes, slice them after soaking.) Add the mushrooms and their soaking water to the strained broth and return to the heat. Add the fish stomach and boil for 30 minutes or so.

Blanch a handful of sliced up bamboo shoots, drain and add to the soup.

Add 2 teaspoons of light Thai soy sauce, 2 teaspoons of Worcestershire sauce and 2 teaspoons of oyster sauce.

Dilute 3 heaping tablespoons of cornflour with enough water to make a thin paste. Slowly add to the broth, stirring all the time, until the broth becomes fairly thick and glistening. Remove from the heat.

Add 200g of shredded chicken (from the one you boiled to make the broth) and about a dozen soft-boiled quails eggs (readily available now in most supermarkets).

Serve the soup with a thin chilli paste made of mashed up fresh red chillies mixed with two pinches of sugar and diluted with white vinegar. (Tiew uses a mortar and pestle to make this chilli seasoning.). Serve the soup in individual bowls and add generous amounts of fine shredded fresh carrot, some fresh coriander leaves and freshly ground pepper. At this point, you can also add a little soy sauce if you feel that the soup needs to be saltier.

SERVES 4-6

NIGHTINGALE FOOD

COSTRADA DE LENGUA

I have adapted this recipe from an 18th-century Spanish cookbook *Nuevo Arte de Cocina* by Juan Altamiras, published in Barcelona in 1758. You can serve this delicious pie as a starter for 8 or as a light main course for 4, accompanied by a mixed-leaf salad, lightly seasoned with balsamic vinegar and good olive oil.

1 ox tongue weighing about 1.2kg
2 cinnamon sticks
Sea salt
400g blanched almonds
225g icing sugar
6 hard boiled egg yolks, mashed
150g unsalted butter
1 x 400g packet of filo pastry
Ground cinnamon for garnish

Put the ox tongue to soak in cold water for an hour or two to clean it of any blood.

Drain the tongue, rinse well and put in a large pot. Cover with water and place over a high heat. As the water comes to the boil, skim it clean, then add the cinnamon sticks and salt to taste. Lower the heat and simmer for $2\frac{1}{2}$ hours, or until the tongue is tender.

Remove the tongue from the cooking broth and, while it is still hot, peel the thick skin off. Set aside.

Pre-heat the oven to 180°C/350°F/Gas 4.

Put the almonds in a food processor and whizz until ground very fine. Transfer to a mixing bowl. Now process the tongue until it too is ground fine. Add the tongue meat to the almonds, together with the sugar, mashed egg yolks and two thirds of the butter. Mix well.

Use a little of the remaining butter to grease a round baking dish measuring 20-25cm in diameter and melt the rest.

Line the dish with one layer of filo pastry, letting the excess hang off the sides. Brush with the melted butter. Lay another sheet of filo and again brush with butter. Repeat until you have used up 6 sheets.

Spread the tongue mixture over the pastry, then fold the excess filo over the filling. Lay 2 or 3 more sheets of filo over, not forgetting to brush them with butter, and tuck the edges underneath the pie.

Bake for 40-50 minutes or until the pastry is crisp and golden. Sprinkle with a little icing sugar and cinnamon and serve immediately.

SERVES 8

CHICKEN LIVER TARTLETS

FOIE DE VOLAILLE EN CASSOLETTE

Here is an unusual but very successful way of using chicken livers. If time is tight and you can't face making the pâté brisée then use ready-baked tartlet cases instead, either small individual ones or mini ones which you can serve as nibbles with drinks.

To make the pâté brisée
125g plain flour
50g butter
1 egg yolk
Pinch fine sea salt
Iced water

To finish
Clarified butter to fry the livers
225g whole organic chicken livers, soaked in milk for 30 minutes
50-75ml red wine
50-75ml chicken stock
50-75ml double cream
Unsalted butter
Sliced black truffle for garnish

Mix all the ingredients for the pâté brisée and knead just enough to bring all the ingredients together. You don't want to develop the gluten. Divide the pastry in 4 pieces and roll out each piece to a circle large enough to line individual, fluted tart cases. Blind bake, in a moderately high oven, using beans to weight the pastry, until crisp and golden brown – about 20-25 minutes.

Melt enough clarified butter to fry the livers in a frying pan. Dry the livers with kitchen paper and sauté long enough for them to crisp on the outside but still remain pink on the inside. Keep warm.

Pour away the butter. Deglaze the pan with the red wine and reduce. Add the chicken stock and reduce again. Add the double cream and bring to the boil. Take off the heat and thicken the sauce with butter.

Divide the chicken livers equally between the tart cases. Cover with the sauce and garnish with the sliced truffle. Serve immediately.

SERVES 4

CHICKEN LIVER MOUSSE

A delightfully light mousse that is perfect when served with tomato sauce and slices of toasted brown bread.

50g unsalted butter
450g organic chicken livers
1 small onion, finely chopped
1 garlic clove, finely chopped
1 teaspoon thyme leaves
1 measure brandy
1 teaspoon finely chopped parsley
1 tablespoon tomato purée
Sea salt and freshly ground pepper
140ml double cream
5 egg whites, stiffly beaten
1 x 30g aspic sachet, diluted in 225ml water

Melt the butter in a large frying pan over a medium heat. When the butter is hot, add the livers, onion, garlic and thyme and cook for 10 minutes, stirring occasionally.

Add the brandy and flame it. Then add the parsley, tomato purée and salt and pepper to taste. Cook for another 5 minutes. Let cool.

Transfer the contents of the pan to a food processor and process until very finely ground. Remove to a mixing bowl. Add the cream and aspic and wait until the mixture starts to set before folding in the egg whites. Spoon into a round or rectangular ceramic mould and refrigerate. Serve slightly chilled with the cold Tomato Sauce (see p124) or, for an unusual combination, with the Crème D' Artichaut (see p124).

SERVES 6-8

SAUTEED CHICKEN LIVERS WITH ARTICHOKES

FEGATINI DE POLLO CON CARCIOFI

A delicious and simple recipe which you can simplify even further by using frozen artichoke hearts.

50g unsalted butter
3 small artichokes, trimmed, boiled, then thinly sliced
500g organic chicken livers
Sea salt and freshly ground black pepper
100g piece of prosciutto, cut across into strips about
　½cm thick
Juice of ½ lemon, or to taste
6 sprigs flat-leaf parsley, bottom stalks discarded,
　then finely chopped

Melt the butter in a large frying pan over a medium heat. Add the artichokes and sauté for 2-3 minutes. Remove onto a plate and keep warm.

Increase the heat to medium-high and add the chicken livers. Cook for 2-3 minutes, turning them to brown evenly, or until they are crisp on the outside but still pink inside. Season with salt and pepper to taste.

Reduce the heat and add the prosciutto and artichokes. Sauté for another minute or so. Add the lemon juice and transfer to a pre-heated serving dish. Garnish with the chopped parsley and serve immediately.

SERVES 4

CALF'S LIVER BRUSCHETTA WITH JUNIPER BUTTER

FOIE DE VEAU AUX TROIS TRANCHES

I love this rather unusual way of serving liver, originally devised by Toulouse Lautrec.
The bruschette take very little time to prepare.
It is very important you use good bread. A mixed wheat pain de campagne with a good crust is my favourite but you can also use a good rye bread or a light wholewheat loaf.

50g softened unsalted butter
1 tablespoon crushed juniper berries
4 slices good bread the size of your hand, each about
   1cm thick
2 slices calf's liver, sliced about 1cm thick, then cut
   across in half
Sea salt and freshly ground pepper to taste
4 medium-thin slices of smoked pancetta

Pre-heat the oven to 230°C/450°F/Gas 8.

Mix the softened butter with the crushed juniper berries. Spread the bread slices equally with most of the butter, saving a little to put on the liver.

Lay the liver slices over the bread. Season with salt and freshly ground pepper to taste, then dot with small knobs of the remaining juniper butter. Lay a slice of smoked pancetta across each and place on a rack.

Bake in the pre-heated oven for 8-12 minutes or until the liver is done to your liking. Serve immediately.

SERVES 4

JERUSALEM MIX BRUSCHETTA

MORAV YORUSHALMI

Jerusalem mix is a typical Israeli street food. It is usually sold in sandwiches or served on a plate with pitta bread accompanied by a a small mezze of chilli and tahini sauces, French fries and pickles. The stalls selling it stay open into the early hours catering for hungry revellers to stop at on their way home after a night out on the town.

1 breast of chicken
6-7 chicken hearts
4 chicken livers
3-4 lamb's kidneys
6 oz rump steak
2 lamb's testicles
2 medium onions, thinly sliced
1 clove garlic, crushed
4 tablespoons extra virgin olive oil
$\frac{1}{2}$ teaspoon ground turmeric
$\frac{1}{2}$ teaspoon curry powder
$\frac{1}{2}$ teaspoon ground coriander
$\frac{1}{2}$ teaspoon sumac
$\frac{1}{2}$ teaspoon ground allspice
$\frac{1}{2}$ teaspoon ground cumin
$\frac{1}{4}$ teaspoon ground cardamom
$\frac{1}{8}$ teaspoon ground cloves
Salt
Freshly ground black pepper
4 slices of good white or brown bread, toasted

Cut the different meats into bite-sized cubes and put in a large mixing bowl. Add the onion, garlic, oil, spices, salt and pepper and mix well. Let marinate for 30 minutes.

Place a large frying pan over a high heat. When the pan is hot, add the meat mixture and sauté for about 5 minutes, or until done to your liking. Spoon equal quantities of the meat mixture onto the toasted bread and serve immediately with pickled hot chillies.

SERVES 4

SAUTEED PIG'S LIVER IN TOMATO SAUCE

FEGATO DI MAIALE AL POMODORO

In Italy, this dish is prepared with pig's liver, but there's no reason why lamb's or chicken's couldn't be used instead. The preparation is the same, except that you cook the lamb's and chicken liver pink, whereas the pig's liver must be cooked through.

4 slices of pig's liver, about 1cm thick
2 bay leaves, crushed to a fine powder
Plain flour, seasoned with salt and pepper
Sea salt and freshly ground pepper, to taste
6 tablespoons extra virgin olive oil
1 small onion, very finely chopped
75ml white wine
1 x 800g tin Italian tomatoes, drained and coarsely
    chopped
A few sprigs flat-leaf parsley, finely chopped

Rub the powdered bay leaves into the liver slices. Dip them in flour. Shake well to remove excess flour and set aside.

Heat half the olive oil in a large frying pan over a medium-high heat. When the oil is hot, sauté the onion until golden. Add the white wine and reduce by more than half. Add the tomatoes and cook for 10-15 minutes or until any excess liquid has evaporated and the sauce has thickened.

While the sauce is cooking, fry the liver in the remaining olive oil over a medium heat for 3-4 minutes on each side, or until completely done.

Transfer the liver onto a serving platter and keep warm. Pour the oil that you used to fry the livers into the tomato sauce and let it bubble for another couple of minutes. Taste and adjust the seasoning if necessary, and pour the sauce over the livers. Garnish with the chopped parsley Serve immediately with plain rice or a green vegetable.

SERVES 4

GAME TOURTE WITH CRANBERRIES

The first time I met Simon Hopkinson was very many years ago, just before he started Bibendum. The late Charles Gray, probably most famous for his role as a James Bond villain, had arranged for him to come and cook lunch at the house of another great friend of mine, Don Munson. Charles had been singing the praises of this young chef and we were all very excited at the prospect of having him prepare something for us at home. The meal was, as promised by Charles, superb. The following recipe is a testament to Hopkinson's talent and is taken from his days as chef at the now defunct, but once highly celebrated, Hilaire in South Kensington.

For the filling
225g game meat (hare, grouse, partridge, etc.)
125g chicken or duck liver
125g pork back fat, cut into tiny dice
125g raw duck foie gras, cut into tiny dice
2 organic eggs
½ teaspoon quatre épices
Sea salt and freshly ground pepper to taste
3 tablespoons port or Madeira

For the tourte
225g puff pastry
1 organic egg, beaten
Home-made or good commercial cranberry sauce

Finely mince the game meat and chicken or duck liver. Transfer to a large mixing bowl and add the remaining ingredients. Mix well. Cover with cling film and refrigerate overnight to let the flavours develop.

Roll out the pastry very thinly and, using a 12.5cm pastry cutter, cut out 8 circles. Transfer 4 discs onto a non-stick baking sheet or one lined with parchment paper.

Pre-heat the oven to 200°C/400°F/Gas 6.

Put a quarter of the filling on each of the 4 pastry circles — make sure you leave about 1.5cm free around the edge. Brush the edges with a little water and lay a pastry circle each over the fillings, aligning the edges. Press all around the edges to seal. Brush with the beaten egg, making sure you don't let the egg dribble over the side — it will stop the pastry from puffing. Bake in the pre-heated oven for 25-35 minutes or until golden all over. Serve hot or warm with cranberry sauce.

SERVES 4

CALF'S LIVER TERRINE

FOIE DE VEAU EN CRÉPINE

You can prepare this terrine in one of two ways; either by chopping the liver in a food processor, though the texture will be too smooth, or ideally by chopping the liver by hand to achieve a rather more chunky, and in my view, better texture. Chicken, lamb or pig's liver can be substituted for calf's. Each terrine will have a different taste, but the finest will be that made with calf's liver. It will also be the most expensive.

25g unsalted butter
1kg calf's liver
9 very thin slices of smoked pancetta
2 organic eggs
2 garlic cloves, crushed
4 shallots, chopped very fine and then crushed with
  a knife
2 teaspoons fine sea salt
Scant $\frac{1}{2}$ teaspoon freshly ground black pepper
Piece of fresh pig's caul, large enough to line the
  terrine dish
A few mint leaves for garnish

Grease the bottom and sides of a medium-sized oval terrine dish (with a tight fitting lid) with butter. Also, grease a sheet of greaseproof paper large enough to cover the top of the terrine with a little butter. Set aside.

Pre-heat the oven to 170°C/325°F/Gas 3.

Chop the liver into very small pieces. The liver should end up like a mash. As you are chopping, discard any nerves or skin. Put the chopped liver in a mixing bowl.

Beat the eggs in a small bowl and stir in the crushed garlic and shallots. Add the egg mixture to the chopped liver. Season with the salt and pepper. Mix well.

Rinse and dry the piece of caul. Line the terrine dish with the caul, choosing the thicker ribbed part for the bottom. Leave quite a bit hanging out, to eventually flap back over the liver. If there are any holes, patch them up by covering with small pieces of caul.

Spread a quarter of the liver mixture over the bottom. Cover with a layer of 3 slices of pancetta. Spread another quarter of liver and repeat until you have 4 layers of liver and 3 of pancetta. Flap over the loose caul.

Cover the terrine with the buttered sheet of greaseproof paper, trimmed to size, and put the lid on. Cook the liver in a bain-marie in the pre-heated oven for $1\frac{1}{4}$-$1\frac{1}{2}$ hours depending on how pink you like it.

When the terrine is ready, carefully pour the cooking juices into a bowl. Strain and reduce the juice to produce a sauce that you will serve with the terrine. Turn out the terrine onto a plate. Line the edge with a few mint leaves and serve hot with the sauce and a potato or parsnip purée. You can also serve the terrine at room temperature with good bread and a salad of your choice.

SERVES 6

CORSICAN BRAWN

U CASGIU DI PORCU

Brawn, known in France as fromage de tête (head cheese), was made in medieval times with wild boar, hence the name, which originally meant the flesh of wild boar. But, as wild boar became rarer in the 16th century, cooks started using pig's heads to make brawn. The old version was a far more spiced dish than the classic modern one. The recipe I give here is from Corsica and is probably closer to that long forgotten medieval boar's brawn.

1 pig's head, boned, singed and washed thoroughly
2 pig's trotters, singed and washed thoroughly
1 onion, quartered
2 cloves garlic, crushed
1 bay leaf
Sea salt
200ml red wine
1 cup chopped flat-leaf parsley
Freshly ground black pepper

Put the head meat and trotters in a large pot. Add the onion, garlic and bay leaf and cover with water. Place over a medium heat and bring to the boil. Skim the water very clean as it comes to the boil, then add salt to taste. Remember that eventually the stock will reduce to ½ litre. Reduce the heat and simmer for 4-5 hours or until the meat is very tender.

Transfer the meat to a bowl. Reserve the trotters for another dish, such as the Mexican Pig's Trotter Salad on p43.

Strain the cooking liquor through a cheese cloth into a clean saucepan and boil over a high heat until you are left with about half a litre.

Chop the head meat into small dice and return to the reduced liquor. Add the wine and season with more salt, if necessary, and pepper. The stock should be full of flavour – there is nothing more disappointing than bland brawn. Simmer for 20 minutes. Remove from the heat and add the parsley. Taste and adjust the seasoning if necessary. Ladle into individual bowls or into a large terrine and refrigerate until the liquor is set.

SERVES 8-12

BRAIN FRITTERS

BEIGNETS DE CERVELLE

These fritters can be made with many kinds of offal, not just brains: blanched sweetbreads, strips of cooked tripe, sections of cooked intestines, strips of cooked ears and so on. In fact, any cut that takes your fancy. You could also go the whole hog and serve a mixture of different cuts for a great offal variation on a fritto misto. You could even forego the batter and simply dip the brain slices in flour and shallow fry them.

For the brains
Juice of 2 lemons, or to taste
8 tablespoons extra virgin olive oil
Few sprigs flat-leaf parsley, finely chopped
Sea salt and freshly ground black pepper
2 calf's brains, blanched, trimmed and sliced

For the batter
225g plain flour
40g cornflour
1/2 tablespoon baking soda
1 tablespoon fine sea salt
310ml sparkling mineral water

To finish
Vegetable oil for frying
1 lemon, quartered

Mix the lemon juice with the oil and most of the parsley (reserve some for garnish), and add salt and pepper to taste. Put the sliced brains to marinate in the mix for a couple of hours.

Half an hour before the brains are ready, combine all the ingredients for the batter. Whisk until the mixture is smooth but do not overwork it — you don't want to develop the gluten. Leave to rest for half an hour

Heat enough vegetable oil to deep-fry the brains in a large frying pan. Make sure the oil is really hot. You can check this by dipping a corner of a brain slice into the oil – if the oil bubbles around it, it is ready.

Remove the brain slices from the marinade. Dip them into the batter and fry until golden on both sides. Remove onto several layers of kitchen paper to drain off the excess fat. When all the slices are fried, transfer to a serving platter. Sprinkle with chopped parsley and serve immediately with the quartered lemon.

SERVES 4-6

BRAINS
IN COCONUT CREAM

GULAI OTAK

Here is a recipe from Indonesia which I found in *Unmentionable Cuisine*, an eccentric book on offal that promotes the idea of eating offal to save the planet! The author, a Mr. Schwabe, doesn't indicate how many people the recipe will serve, nor does he give precise instructions, but the dish is good and unusual so I have reproduced it here verbatim.

Brown a chopped onion in oil and add a blanched brain cut into large pieces. Also add ground pepper, turmeric, salt and chopped mint; cover with coconut cream. Simmer for 20 minutes.

Another recipe from the same book reminded me of an amazingly delicate brain mousse that I enjoyed recently in one of Rome's best restaurants. The following preparation is Norwegian and is called Hrerneboller.

Put a blanched brain through the finest blade of a food chopper along with its weight of white bread. Mix in crushed garlic, an egg, lemon juice, chopped parsley, salt and pepper. Form into small dumplings and poach.

WARM CHICKEN LIVER SALAD
WITH BALSAMIC VINEGAR

It was at a huge food fair that I first tried this salad. The stand belonged to a balsamic vinegar producer, and he had a chef churning out platefuls of the salad to show the versatility of balsamic vinegar.

3 tablespoons extra virgin olive oil
500g organic chicken livers
1 tablespoon good, aged, balsamic vinegar
Sea salt and freshly ground black pepper to taste
1 x 225g packet mixed leaf salad

Put the oil in a frying pan and place over a medium-high heat. When the oil is hot, add the livers and sauté until crisp on the outside but still pink on the inside. Take off the heat and immediately add the balsamic vinegar and salt and pepper to taste. Mix well.

Divide the salad equally between 4 plates. Arrange equal quantities of livers over the greens and drizzle a little sauce all over. Serve immediately with good bread.

SERVES 4

MOROCCAN BRAIN SALAD

L'MOKH M'CHERMAL

Put all the ingredients, apart from the brains, in a saucepan and simmer for 20 minutes, stirring occasionally, until the sauce thickens.

Blanch the brains in salted water and trim them. Add the brains to the sauce and simmer for 5-10 minutes, carefully turning from time to time. Serve warm or at room temperature.

SERVES 4-6

You could substitute the brains here by using lamb's liver, which you will need to sauté first. Moroccans sometimes add to the richness of this dish by frying eggs in the sauce, or alternatively they make it fresher by adding petits pois.

4 tablespoons extra virgin olive oil
4-6 garlic cloves, crushed
1 x 400g Italian tin tomatoes, finely chopped
4 tablespoons chopped flat-leaf parsley
3 tablespoons wine vinegar
2$\frac{1}{2}$ teaspoons ground cumin
1 tablespoon paprika
Pinch saffron threads
Sea salt to taste
5 lamb's brains, soaked for 30 minutes in cold water, then cut in half

LAMB'S TONGUE SALAD

SALATET L'SANAT

There is always a surreal moment when, as I bite into a lamb's tongue, I feel as if I am biting into a lover's tongue. This fleeting sensation has never put me off eating tongue, lamb's or ox's, and nor should it you.

8 lamb's tongues (about 750g)
The peel of half a lemon
2 cinnamon sticks
$\frac{1}{2}$ tablespoon sea salt
1 x 225g mixed leaf salad

Put the tongues to soak for an hour or two to clean them of any blood. Drain, rinse well and put in a large pot. Cover with about 750ml water and place over high heat. As the water comes to the boil, skim it clean then add the lemon peel, cinnamon sticks and salt. Reduce the heat to medium-low and simmer for 45 minutes or until the tongues are tender.

Prepare the vinaigrette on page 128.

When the tongues are ready, remove them from the cooking broth and peel the skin from them while still hot. Pat the tongues dry and cut in half lengthways, being careful not to separate the halves. You need to be able to open them out and lay them flat without actually dividing them. Dress the salad and transfer to a flat serving dish. Arrange the tongues over the greens, cut side up. Serve immediately.

SERVES 4-6

KIDNEY SALAD
IN SESAME SAUCE

LIANGBAN ZHIMA YAOZ

Innards are considered a great delicacy in the Szechwanese countryside and are served only on special occasions. The following recipe comes from a wonderful cookbook by Mrs Chiang. It is very simple and quick to prepare and provides an unusual and tasty starter.

6 pork kidneys
3 tablespoons Chinese rice wine
8 cloves garlic, peeled and coarsely chopped
5cm piece fresh ginger, peeled and coarsely chopped
Fine sea salt
3 spring onions, trimmed and thinly sliced
$\frac{1}{2}$ teaspoon caster sugar
2 teaspoons chilli flakes in oil
$\frac{1}{2}$ teaspoon rice wine vinegar
$1\frac{1}{2}$ tablespoons soy sauce
1 teaspoon sesame paste
1 teaspoon sesame oil
$\frac{1}{2}$ teaspoon roasted and ground Szechwan
   peppercorns

Slice each kidney in half lengthwise. Remove and discard the core. Lightly score the outside of each piece, making small diamond shapes. Slice thinly. Transfer to a bowl and cover with cold water. Let soak for 15 minutes. The soaking helps get rid of the strong smell and taste of the kidneys.

Drain the kidney slices and put to soak again, but this time in the rice wine, for 10 minutes.

Put the garlic, ginger and $\frac{1}{2}$ teaspoon of salt in a mortar and pound with a pestle until you have a smooth paste.

Bring 500ml water to boil in a saucepan. Add the kidney slices and simmer for 3 minutes. It is important you don't overcook the kidneys or else they will become rubbery. Drain and rinse under cold water.

Put the cooked kidneys in a bowl and add the garlic-ginger paste, the onion and seasonings. Mix well and serve immediately. Or refrigerate to serve later, making sure you stir the kidneys well before serving.

SERVES 6

MEXICAN PIG'S TROTTER SALAD

This refreshing recipe comes from Frida Kahlo, or at least from a book of her recipes and reminiscences. It is great to serve on a picnic on a hot summer's day.

4 pig's trotters, singed and cleaned
1 small onion, studded with 2 cloves
1 garlic clove
4 peppercorns
1 bay leaf
Sea salt

For the marinade
200ml white wine vinegar
$1/2$ teaspoon finely ground white pepper
2 teaspoons fresh thyme leaves

For the salsa
500g ripe fresh tomatoes, peeled, seeded and coarsely
    chopped
1 small Spanish onion, very finely chopped
$1^1/_2$ teaspoons dried oregano
Chilli flakes
2-3 tablespoons coriander, finely chopped for garnish

Place the pig's trotters in a large pot. Add the onion, garlic, pepper and bay leaf. Cover with water, about $1^1/_2$ litres, and bring to the boil over a medium heat. As the water is about to boil, skim the surface clean and add $1^1/_2$ tablespoons of sea salt. Lower the heat and barely simmer for 3 hours or until the trotters are done. Leave the trotters to cool a little in their cooking broth.

Mix the ingredients for the marinade together.

Put the tomatoes, chopped onion and oregano in a mixing bowl. Add salt and chilli flakes to taste and mix well. Set aside.

When the trotters have cooled, take them out of their cooking broth. Rinse and pat them dry. Cut them in half lengthways and carefully remove the bones, or as many as you can without tearing the meat. Put the meat to marinate in the vinegar mixture for two hours, turning occasionally.

Drain off the meat and discard the marinade. Transfer to a serving dish and cover with the salsa. Sprinkle with the coriander and serve either at room temperature or chilled.

SERVES 2

STUFFED PIG'S TROTTERS

PIEDS DE PORCS FARCIS TRUFFÉS

Ideally you should use fresh or frozen truffles – black truffles freeze remarkably well. However, if you can't get either, then use canned ones. You could even omit them altogether, though the way they are laid in a line underneath the caul makes for an appealing presentation.

2 pig's trotters, singed and thoroughly washed
1 medium onion, studded with 2 cloves
Bouquet garni (bay, thyme and parsley)
Sea salt
12 black peppercorns
50g black truffle
300g minced lean pork meat, preferably from the filet
100g minced pork fat
¼ teaspoon finely ground white pepper
4 square pieces caul, each about 20cm square
Lard
Fresh breadcrumbs

Place the trotters in a large pot. Cover with 3.5 litres water. Add the onion, bouquet garni, 2 tablespoons of sea salt and the peppercorns. Bring to the boil, then reduce the heat and simmer gently for about 3 hours or until the feet are done.

Brush and peel the truffle, if you are using it. Keep the peel and slice the truffle into medium-thin discs. You don't want to make the slices too thin or they will burn under the grill. Cover and set aside.

Put the minced meat and fat in a mixing bowl. Chop the truffle peel and add to the meat. Season with 2 teaspoons salt and the white pepper. Mix well.

When the trotters are done, let them cool a little in the cooking broth before removing onto a chopping board. Cut them in half lengthways. Carefully remove the bones, including the tiny ones that are buried into the flesh — try not to tear the meat. Slice the trotters into long strips about 1cm wide, and divide the sliced meat in 4 equal portions. Set aside.

Lay out a clean kitchen cloth over your work surface and spread a piece of caul over it. If there are any holes, cover these with smaller pieces of caul.

Divide the truffle slices in eight parts. Arrange one part in a line down the middle of the caul. Divide the minced meat mixture in 8 equal parts. With one part, make a rectangular pattie about 14cm long by 6cm wide. Lay the meat over the truffles. making sure the truffles are in the middle, and flatten evenly.

Place one part of the trotter slices in an even layer over the meat. If the slices are too long, fold the ends over the meat. Cover with another layer of flattened minced meat. Then arrange a truffle part down the middle, and wrap the caul around the meat to make a neat rectangular parcel. Be sure to encase the stuffing well. The stuffed trotter should have rounded ends and be about 2.5cm thick.

Turn your grill on low. Make the rest of the stuffed trotters and delicately rub them all with a little lard. Grill under a very moderate heat, so that the stuffing cooks through, for 10 minutes on each side. Serve on pre-heated plates.

SERVES 4

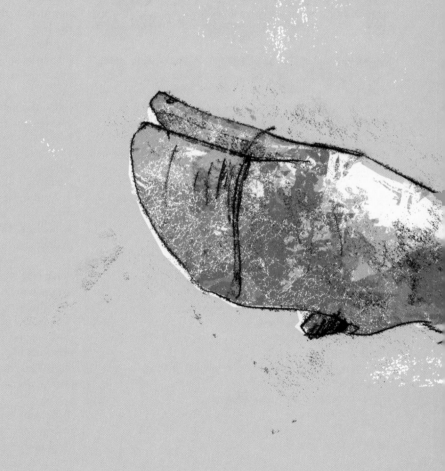

ABALONE AND GOOSE FEET
COOKED WITH GRAVY IN A CLAY CONTAINER

I have included the following recipe by Lee Kui, from *Cooking with Honk Kong's Top Chefs*, more to be read than cooked. I can buy huge sacks of frozen chicken feet in any Chinese supermarket in London but I have yet to find goose feet for sale. And even if I were to find them, I am not sure I would know how to bone the feet, but that's not to say that the enthusiastic reader shouldn't have a go!

4 pairs goose feet, deboned and washed
2 pieces sliced ginger
2 spring onions
1/4 piece aged orange peel
2 star anise
1/2 cup abalone soup
250ml chicken stock
2 tablespoons oyster sauce
Few drops sesame oil
1 teaspoon sugar
1 teaspoon cornflour
1 teaspoon mild rice wine
150g abalone, cut in 1/2cm slices

Blanch the goose feet in boiling water for 3 minutes. Drain and transfer to a heavy-bottomed saucepan. Add the ginger, onion, orange peel, star anise and abalone soup together with 250ml of water and chicken stock. Place over low heat and simmer for 1 1/2 hours.

Mix the oyster sauce with the sesame oil, sugar, cornflour and rice wine.

When the feet are ready, remove the ginger, onion, orange peel and star anise. Stir in the oyster sauce mixture and add the abalone. Transfer to a serving dish. Sprinkle with a little rice wine.
Serve immediately.

SERVES 4

SAUTEED SPLEEN

T'HAL

T'hal is one of my favourite dishes. Whenever I go back to Beirut to visit my mother, I have a list of Lebanese dishes that I want her to prepare for me, and T'hal is always one of them (as is Ghammeh on page 96). The texture of the spleen is so melting and the taste of the thick, dark sauce so moreish that my mouth is watering as I write this recipe.

2 heads garlic (about 18-20 cloves), crushed
100g coriander, most of the bottom stalk discarded, then finely chopped
1 teaspoon ground coriander
$1/8$ teaspoon cayenne pepper
Sea salt to taste
1 ox spleen
2-3 tablespoons extra virgin olive oil
75ml red wine vinegar
75ml lemon juice
$1/2$ teaspoon seven-pepper mixture (or ground allspice)
Scant $1/4$ teaspoon ground cinnamon

Mix the crushed garlic and chopped coriander in a mixing bowl. Add the ground coriander, cayenne pepper and salt to taste. Mix well and set aside.

Remove any loose skin or fat from the spleen and cut it across into two equal pieces. Slide your knife inside the flesh, at the thickest part of the spleen, and make long slits. Fill these with as much garlic/coriander mixture as you can, using your finger to push the filling in.

Put the olive oil in a large saucepan and place over a medium-high heat. When the oil is hot, add the spleen and brown it on both sides – about 7 minutes each side.

Add the seven-pepper mixture (or allspice), the cinnamon and salt to taste. Pour in half the lemon juice and half the vinegar. Reduce the heat to medium-low, cover the pan and simmer for a few minutes. As the sauce reduces and thickens, add more lemon juice and vinegar, a little at a time, until you have used up both. This should take 15-20 minutes. Turn the meat regularly during this time.

Reduce the heat to very low and simmer for another 20-30 minutes, checking on the sauce to make sure it is not becoming too dry. If it is, add a little water, not too much though, as you want the sauce to be very concentrated. Take off the heat and leave to cool. Serve warm or at room temperature.

SERVES 4-6

MOROCCAN STUFFED SPLEEN

TEYHAN

This is the Moroccan way to prepare spleen. As with the Lebanese version, the spleen is stuffed, though the stuffing is far more substantial and meaty, consisting as it does of liver and heart. You find Teyhan on the food stalls of Jame' el-Fna in Marrakesh, though I have never plucked up the courage to try it there. Luckily, a friend made it for me on one of my visits to Morocco, and then later I tried it in a number of small cafés. The home-made version was better and here is my friend's recipe.

500g lamb's liver, cut into very small pieces
1 lamb's heart, cut into very small pieces
5 garlic cloves, crushed
8 sprigs coriander, most of the stalk discarded,
  then finely chopped
1 teaspoon ground cumin
2 teaspoons paprika
Sea salt to taste
4 tablespoons extra virgin olive oil, plus more to brush
  the spleen and grease the roasting dish
1 ox spleen

Pre-heat the oven to 180°C/350°F/Gas 4.

Put the liver and heart in a large mixing bowl. Add the garlic, coriander, seasonings and oil and mix well.

Make a deep slit in the spleen all along the side, cutting almost all the way to the other side, but being careful not to let the knife cut right through. Insert the meat filling in the cavity and brush the spleen with a little oil.

Place the spleen in a roasting dish, which you have brushed with a little olive oil. Roast in the pre-heated oven for 40 minutes, or until cooked through. Serve immediately.

SERVES 4-6

SWEETBREAD BOREKS

I was given the following recipe by my friend Elisabeth Luard, author of *European Peasant Cookery*. If you are feeling too lazy to make boreks, then just use the filling to make crostini. Simply rub the toasted bread with a cut garlic clove, drizzle a little olive oil over it and spread with the sweetbread mixture.

750g lamb's sweetbreads
Juice of $\frac{1}{2}$ a lemon
Sea salt
A few sprigs each of parsley and coriander, with most
   of the stalk discarded, and finely chopped
Half a handful of chives, finely chopped
A few sprigs of oregano, leaves only
$1\frac{1}{2}$ tablespoons extra virgin olive oil
Freshly ground pepper to taste
Lemon wedges, to serve

To finish
16 sheets of filo pastry (each about 32 x 18cm)
100g unsalted butter, melted

Soak the sweetbreads in cold water for about 1 hour. Drain and rinse until the water runs clear. Remove as much skin and fatty bits as you can without damaging the sweetbreads.

Put the sweetbreads in a pan and cover with cold water. Add the lemon juice and a little salt and bring to boil over a medium-high heat. As soon as the water comes to the boil, drain the sweetbreads and dry with kitchen paper.

Chop up the meat very small and transfer to a mixing bowl. Add the rest of the ingredients and mix well. Taste and adjust the seasoning, if necessary.

Place a sheet of filo pastry on your work surface. Brush with melted butter and fold in half lengthways. Brush again with melted butter. Place $1\frac{1}{2}$-2 tablespoons of filling about 2cm away from the edge of the pastry. Take a corner of the pastry and fold the filo over the filling to form a triangle. Fold again, aligning the edges together to continue with the triangle shape. Fold again and again, brushing with butter every two or three folds, until you reach the end of the strip of filo. Make the remaining boreks in the same way.

Once you have finished making the boreks, you can either deep-fry them in hot vegetable oil until golden brown all over, or bake them, as I do, in a pre-heated oven at 180°C/350°F/Gas 4 for 15-20 minutes, or until the triangles are crisp and golden all over. Serve immediately with wedges of lemon.

MAKES 16 BOREKS

MORSEDDU ON TOAST

BRUSCHETTE DI MORSEDDU

Morseddu is a Calabrian speciality. The name comes from the Italian verb morsi, meaning to bite – the dish has this name because it is quite chewy. I have always thought it a great shame that pig's liver is not more generally appreciated, as it is really very good to eat. As for the lungs and hearts, they too are unfairly neglected and consequently not readily available – so you will need to order them from your butcher a day or two ahead of cooking.

100ml extra virgin olive oil
300g pig's liver, cut into 1cm slices
200g pig's lungs, diced into small cubes
200g pig's heart, diced into small cubes
2 cloves garlic, finely chopped
3 x 400g tins Italian canned tomatoes, drained,
   and chopped
$1/4$ teaspoon chilli flakes
Sea salt and freshly ground black pepper

To finish
6 slices good country bread, toasted
Few sprigs flat-leaf parsley, finely chopped

Heat the olive oil in a saucepan over a medium heat. When the oil is hot, add the meats and sauté for a couple of minutes, or until browned.

Reduce the heat and add the garlic, tomatoes and seasonings and simmer for 30 minutes. Taste and adjust the seasoning, if necessary. Spoon equal quantities of meat and sauce onto the toast and garnish with the chopped parsley. Serve immediately.

SERVES 6

CALF'S FEET SALAD

NERVETTI IN INSALATA

The Italians generally buy calf's feet salad ready-prepared from their wonderful food shops, such as the glorious Peck in Milan. However, I suspect that sourcing prepared calf's feet will be something of a challenge in Britain and America, unless you are lucky enough to find a willing supplier. I have eaten them diced into big squares in restaurants in Rome but I really prefer them thinly sliced. Sometimes in Italy you will find cooked cannellini beans added to the nervetti.

2 small red onions, finely chopped
2 tablespoons white wine vinegar
2 calf's feet, scraped, singed and cleaned very well
1 medium onion, quartered
1 medium carrot, cut in chunks
1 celery stalk, cut in chunks
4 tablespoons extra virgin olive oil
1 tablespoon chopped flat-leaf parsley
Sea salt and freshly ground black pepper

Put the red onions to soak in the vinegar.

Place the calf's feet in a large pot. Add the quartered onion, carrot and celery and cover well with water. Place over a medium-high heat and bring to the boil. As the water comes to the boil, skim it clean. Add salt to taste. Then reduce the heat to low and simmer for 2 hours, or until the meat comes away easily from the bone. Drain the feet and allow to cool. When cool take the meat off the bone and slice thinly into long strips.

Transfer the meat to a salad bowl. Strain the onions soaked in vinegar, reserving the vinegar, and add to the meat.

Make a dressing by adding the oil to the vinegar – you may think that there is too much vinegar, in which case reduce the amount. Add salt and pepper to taste and whisk together. Add the dressing to the meat and onions, together with the chopped parsley, and mix well. Serve with good white bread.

SERVES 4

MAIN
DISHES &
FEASTS

OXTAIL
BUTCHER STYLE

CODA BI BUE ALLA VACCINARA

This is one of the most typical of Roman offal dishes and one you would certainly find at one of Rome's most celebrated offal restaurants, Il Cecchino. Renowned for its Coda di Bue, the restaurant is situated next to the wonderful Testaccio market. This version is a little more elaborate than the one served at Il Cecchino.

1 tablespoon lard
2kg oxtail, cut into pieces across each vertebra
1 medium onion, finely chopped
1 leek, white part only, thinly sliced
1 carrot, thinly sliced
1 bouquet garni made up of 2 sprigs thyme,
   a few sprigs of parsley and 1 bay leaf
Sea salt and pepper grains

To finish
3 tablespoons extra virgin olive oil
1 medium onion, finely chopped
100g prosciutto in one piece, sliced into thin strips
200ml white wine
1 x 800g Italian tin tomatoes, drained and coarsely
   chopped
1 heart of celery, cut into 2cm pieces
1 teaspoon dried oregano
$\frac{1}{4}$ teaspoon ground cinnamon
Pinch grated nutmeg
30g pine nuts, sautéed in a little butter
50g sultanas

Put the lard, oxtail and vegetables in a large pot and place over a medium heat. Sauté until the meat has browned and the vegetables softened.

Cover with water, about $1\frac{1}{2}$ litres, and add the bouquet garni, together with $1\frac{1}{2}$ tablespoons of salt and 6 pepper grains. As the water comes to the boil, skim the surface clean. Then lower the heat and simmer for 2 hours.

Put the olive oil and onion in a sauté pan, large enough to eventually take the oxtail, and fry over a medium-high heat until the onion turns golden. Add the prosciutto, stir for a few seconds, then pour in the wine. Reduce the liquid by three quarters. Add the tomatoes, celery, oregano, cinnamon and nutmeg. Cook for 20-25 minutes, stirring occasionally, until the tomato sauce is thickened.

When the oxtail is ready, remove it from the stock. Pat the pieces dry with kitchen paper and drop into the tomato sauce. Add 200ml of the stock, making sure that you skim it of all fat. Simmer, covered, for another hour, stirring occasionally and adding a little stock if the sauce becomes too dry.

Finally add the pine nuts and raisins, and season with salt and pepper to taste. Simmer for another 10 minutes. Taste and adjust the seasoning, if necessary. Serve very hot.

SERVES 6

ARABELLA BOXER'S BRAISED OXTAIL

Even though Arabella Boxer is a great friend, it was another close friend, Patricia Pollen, who first made this dish for me. Though the preparation is quite time consuming – you will need to start a day ahead – the actual cooking is very simple. Arabella Boxer recommends it as 'a wonderful winter dish, sustaining without being too expensive.' I agree.

1st day

2 oxtail, cut in 5cm sections, trimmed of excess fat
2½ tablespoons plain flour, seasoned with sea salt
   and freshly ground black pepper
2 tablespoons extra virgin olive oil
30g unsalted butter
2 cloves garlic, crushed
2 tablespoons tomato purée
1 large onion, cut in half
1 large carrot, cut in half
1 bay leaf
3 stalks parsley
720ml beef stock
150ml red wine

2nd day

30g unsalted butter
1 tablespoon extra virgin olive oil
1 leek, cut in thick strips
2 medium carrots, cut in thick strips
2 small turnips, cut in thick strips
2 stalks celery, cut in thick strips
2 tablespoons coarsely chopped parsley

Put the meat in a large bowl and shake the seasoned flour over it. Turn the meat to coat it all over.

Pre-heat the oven to 150°C/300°F/Gas 2.

Put the oil and butter in a large braising pot and place over a medium heat. Add the oxtail and brown all over.

Add the garlic and tomato purée together with the halved vegetables, stock and wine. Bring to the boil, cover and place in the pre-heated oven. Cook for 4 hours. Remove from the oven and leave to cool overnight.

The following day, remove all the fat from the surface and transfer the pieces of oxtail to a shallow earthenware dish. Discard the vegetables and herbs.

Pre-heat the oven to 180°C/350°F/Gas 4.

Heat the butter and oil in a sauté pan. Add the vegetable strips and fry gently for 8 minutes. Add the oxtail stock and simmer gently for 15 minutes. Taste and adjust the seasoning, if necessary. Pour the stock and vegetables over the oxtail and cook in the pre-heated oven for 1 hour, basting from time to time, until the meat is slightly crisp and caramelised where it peeps out of the juices. Garnish with the chopped parsley. Serve very hot with boiled potatoes and a green salad.

SERVES 6

JAMAICAN OXTAIL IN RED WINE
WITH BIRD'S EYE CHILLIES

I lived for a while next to the most wonderful Jamaican man who, every now and then, used to hand me a bowl of oxtail stew on a bed of rice over the garden fence. It was quite delicious. Unfortunately John moved back to Jamaica long before I started working on this book and I never got round to asking him for exact instructions on how to make the stew. So I looked for an alternative recipe and found one in Cristine Mackie's book on Carribbean food, *Life and Food in the Caribbean*. Here is how hers is made.

2-3 tablespoons coconut oil
750g oxtail
1 bird's eye chilli
2 medium onions, finely chopped
1 tablespoon chopped celery
2 mild chilli peppers
1 whole head garlic, cut in half
Sea salt and freshly ground black pepper
120ml tomato ketchup
120ml good red wine

Put the coconut oil in a large sauté pan and place over a medium-high heat. Add the oxtail and the chilli and brown the oxtail, taking great care not to let the chilli burst.

Add the onions, celery, peppers and garlic. Season with salt and pepper to taste and cook, stirring occasionally, until the onion has softened.

Stir in the ketchup and let it bubble for a few seconds. Then add the wine and let it bubble for a minute or so. Stir in 120ml water. Reduce the heat to low and simmer, covered, for a couple of hours, or until the meat falls off the bone. Check on the sauce every now and then to see that it doesn't dry out. If it gets too dry, add a little water. Taste and adjust the seasoning at the end of cooking. Remove the bird's eye chilli and serve very hot, accompanied with plain rice.

SERVES 4

OXTAIL IN ASPIC

QUEUE DE BEUF EN GELÉE

Here is a wonderful summer dish which I learned
from my great friend Anne-Marie. The preparation
is very simple although the cooking time is fairly long.
Ask your butcher to tie the oxtail sections in a bundle
the way French butchers do it.

3 medium onions, cut in half
2 carrots, cut in chunks
2 leeks, trimmed and cut in chunks
2 turnips, cut in half
1 celery heart, cut in chunks
Few sprigs flat-leaf parsley
Few sprigs thyme
2-3 sprigs rosemary
2-3 bay leaves
Few peppercorns
Sea salt
1 oxtail
6 sheets gelatine, about 18g
1 small bunch tarragon, leaves only

Put the vegetables, herbs and seasonings in a large
pot. Add 3 litres of water and place over a medium
heat. Simmer for 1 hour.

Add the oxtail and simmer for another 2 hours, or
until the meat falls off the bone. Remove the oxtail
and let it cool a little before taking the meat off the
bone, discarding the skin and any gelatinous bits.
The meat will automatically break into smallish
pieces. Cover and set aside.

Remove the vegetables from the broth and discard.
Strain the broth through cheesecloth and refrigerate
until the fat forms a solid layer on the surface.
Skim the fat and measure 800 ml stock.

Break up the gelatine sheets and soak in
3-4 tablespoons of water for 5 minutes.

Heat the measured stock and add to the gelatine.
Whisk the stock until the gelatine is completely
diluted. Stir in the meat and tarragon (reserve a
few leaves for garnish) and pour the mixture into
a medium bowl – you will eventually need to turn
out the jellied oxtail, so, choose a nice, easy shape.
Refrigerate the oxtail until the liquid is set.
This will take around 3 hours. Then dip the bowl in
boiling water for 30 seconds or so to loosen the aspic.
Turn out the set oxtail onto a plate. Decorate with a
few tarragon leaves. Serve with a mixed leaf salad.

SERVES 6

OX TONGUE
WITH FRESH TOMATO SAUCE

LANGUE DE BOEUF SAUCE TOMATE

If you were to buy this dish ready-made in Paris, the sauce would probably be made with tomato purée, but without either the capers or the cornichons. I much prefer the fresh tasting sauce in the recipe below, which was given to me by a great butcher-tripier in Paris, Mr. Guérin, who, during the time I was testing recipes there, supplied me with all the offal I needed.

1 ox tongue, weighing about 1.2kg
1 onion, studded with 3 cloves
1 carrot, trimmed and quartered
1 branch celery with leaves on
1 leek, trimmed
1 bouquet garni (thyme, laurel and parsley)
8 peppercorns
Sea salt to taste
Tomato sauce (page 123)

Put the ox tongue to soak in cold water for 1-2 hours to clean it of any blood. Drain, rinse and put in a large pot. Cover with water and place over a high heat. As the water comes to the boil, skim it clean. Add the vegetables and seasonings. Lower the heat and simmer for 2½ hours, or until the tongue is tender.

Prepare the tomato sauce.

When the tongue is done, peel the skin off it while it is still hot. Cut into medium-thick slices and transfer to a pre-heated serving dish. Pour the hot tomato sauce all over and serve immediately with boiled new potatoes.

SERVES 6-8

OX TONGUE
IN SWEET-SOUR SAUCE

LINGUA DI BUE IN AGRO-DOLCE

Here is a rather unusual but very appealing way to prepare tongue that suits perfectly the soft, lean texture of the meat. A speciality from the centre of Italy, Lingua di Bue in Agro-Dolce is normally served with rice, but steamed couscous, although totally unorthodox, also makes an excellent accompaniment. You can also serve it on its own with good bread.

1 ox tongue weighing about 1.2kg
50g unsalted butter
1 small onion, finely chopped
1 small carrot, finely chopped
1 bay leaf
1 tablespoon raw cane sugar
30g unsweetened plain chocolate, grated
200ml red wine vinegar
1 tablespoon flour
300ml dark meat stock
100g stoned prunes
75g pine nuts
150g pitted sour cherries
100g sultanas
3 tablespoons mixed candied fruit, diced into
   small cubes
Sea salt and freshly ground black pepper

Prepare, cook and peel the tongue, as indicated in the previous recipe.

Melt the butter in a large sauté pan over a medium heat. Add the chopped onion, carrot and bay leaf and fry until lightly coloured. Add the sugar and chocolate and stir until melted. Pour in the vinegar and boil for a couple of minutes.

Whisk the flour into the stock and slowly incorporate it into the vinegar sauce.

Add the prunes and simmer for 10 minutes. Add the rest of the ingredients and season with salt and pepper to taste. Be sure to use salt sparingly so as not to disturb the delicate balance between sweet and sour. Simmer for a further 5 minutes.

When the tongue is ready, slice it and add to the sauce. Heat through without letting the sauce boil. Taste and adjust the seasoning, if necessary. Serve very hot.

SERVES 4-6

OX
TONGUE STEW WITH POTATOES

ROSTO

I always felt that this Lebanese dish had its inspiration in French cooking, and when I was given the classic French recipe for ox tongue on page 58, my suspicions grew stronger. It was probably during the years of the French protectorate that the Lebanese came across French ox tongue in tomato sauce and, given their taste for all things foreign, they must have happily adopted it and added it to their own repertoire. Then, as always happens with recipes that are adopted, they would have changed it to suit their taste by making use of their own traditional spices. Then, probably because of seasonal supply, they must have skipped fresh tomatoes in favour of tomato purée and finally replaced the cornichons and capers with potatoes and garlic, to produce a very different dish with a spicier, heavier sauce that is now very much their own.

1 ox tongue weighing 1.2kg
3 cinnamon sticks
3 medium onions, one left whole and the others quartered
Sea salt
2 teaspoons Lebanese seven-pepper mixture (or ground allspice)
½ teaspoon finely ground black pepper
¼ teaspoon ground cinnamon
20 garlic cloves
50g unsalted butter
2 tablespoons vegetable oil
1 x 140g can tomato purée
1.5kg medium-sized potatoes, peeled and quartered

Soak the ox tongue in several changes of cold water for a couple of hours to get rid of any blood. Drain and rinse well. Put in a large pot. Add one cinnamon stick, the whole onion and a little salt. Bring to the boil over a moderate heat. As the water comes to the boil, skim it clean. Simmer for 1 hour, then remove the tongue from the cooking broth and peel off the thick skin while the tongue is still hot.

Mix all the spices together, adding a little salt to taste. Dip half the garlic cloves into the spice mixture. Make 10 slits all over the tongue and insert the seasoned garlic cloves into the cavities.

Put the butter and oil in a large clean pan and place over a medium-high heat. Add the tongue and brown it on all sides. Transfer the tongue to a plate.

Add the quartered onions and garlic to the pan. Sauté for 5-10 minutes, or until softened and lightly golden. Return the tongue to the pan and strain enough broth over it to just cover. Add the remaining cinnamon sticks and salt to taste, and boil for a further hour.

Remove the cinnamon sticks. Add the tomato purée, potatoes and spices. Reduce the heat to medium and boil gently for another 20 minutes, or until the potatoes are done and the sauce thickened. Taste and adjust the seasoning if necessary. Serve very hot with plain rice or just good country bread.

SERVES 6-8

TAGINE
OF OX TONGUE

L'SANE M'QALLI

Here is a recipe that I found in a fascinating book, *La Cuisine Marocaine de Rabat*, by Hayat Dinia. Offal is highly prized in Morocco. And if you walk around the weekly souks outside Marrakesh, you will more than likely trip over unskinned calf's or sheep's heads leering at you from the dusty floors in between the butchers' stalls, their tongues sticking out at the sides of their mouths making them seem ghoulishly alive. When you then lift your eyes to the stalls themselves, hoping for some respite from the grizzly sight below, you recoil even further as intestines and stomachs hang from meat hooks directly before your eyes. It all makes for a perfectly ghastly setting for a horror film. However, scary or not, all this offal is used to produce fabulous and surprisingly refined dishes. One of my particular favourites is M'assal (calf's' feet cooked in spices and honey). Another is Calf's Feet Cooked with Chickpeas and Wheat (page 69), which the Moroccans eat on the street for breakfast but which I prefer to have for lunch. The following tagine is very simple to prepare and the end result wonderful.

1 ox tongue weighing about 1kg, well cleaned
500g cannellini beans, soaked overnight with
   1 teaspoon bicarbonate of soda
4 tablespoons extra virgin olive oil
1 tablespoon paprika
2 teaspoons ground cumin
Sea salt
6-8 garlic cloves, crushed
2 tablespoons wine vinegar

Boil the ox tongue in plenty of salted water for 10-15 minutes. Remove from the heat and peel. Cut into medium-thick slices and put in a saucepan.

Drain and rinse the beans. Add them to the tongue together with the other ingredients, except for the vinegar. Add $1\frac{1}{2}$ litres of water and boil gently for about $1\frac{1}{2}$ hours, or until the meat and pulses are tender and the sauce reduced. Check on the sauce half way through cooking to see that it is not drying out. If the sauce is too thin at the end of cooking, increase the heat and boil hard until reduced. Transfer the tongue and beans to a serving dish. Sprinkle with the vinegar and serve immediately with good bread.

SERVES 6

STUFFED
AND BRAISED CALF'S HEART

COEUR DE VEAU FARCI AND BRAISÉ

I doubt if all that many people in England or certainly America have ever eaten heart. Most assume that it is only good for dog or cat food. A mistaken assumption. Heart may not be the finest part of an animal to eat but it is good and cheap to buy. The texture is firm but not chewy and the taste slightly gamey. Calf's and lamb's hearts are finer than ox's or even pig's. You can prepare heart in many different ways; stuffed and braised as below, or simply cut into medium-thin steaks and fried in a little butter, or even cut into cubes and then seasoned and threaded onto skewers ready to be barbecued.

1 large onion, thinly sliced
4-6 sprigs flat-leaf parsley, coarsely chopped
2 sprigs thyme, leaves only
1 bay leaf
200ml white wine
2 tablespoons extra virgin olive oil
2 calf's hearts weighing about 600g each
Sea salt and freshly ground black pepper

For the stuffing
25g unsalted butter
1 small onion, finely chopped
200g finely ground sausage meat
4-6 sprigs flat-leaf parsley, finely chopped
2 tablespoons stale breadcrumbs, soaked in
   a little stock
1 organic egg
1/2 teaspoon grated nutmeg

To finish
Piece of caul large enough to wrap the hearts
30g unsalted butter
1 tablespoon flour
250ml meat or vegetable stock
1 tablespoon tomato purée

Mix the onion, herbs, white wine and olive oil in a large mixing bowl. Add the hearts and season with salt and pepper. Leave for 2 hours, turning regularly.

Melt the butter for the stuffing in a frying pan and sauté the onion until lightly coloured. Transfer to a mixing bowl. Add the sausage meat together with the parsley, bread, nutmeg, and salt and pepper to taste. Mix well and set aside.

Divide the stuffing in two equal parts. Fill each heart with the mince – hearts always come slit open because meat inspectors have to check that they are healthy. Pack the meat in the cavities. Close the hearts and wrap each tightly with a piece of caul. Tie loosely with a few rounds of thread.

Pre-heat the oven to 150°C/300°F/Gas 2.

Melt the butter in an oval braising pan over a medium heat. When the butter is hot, brown the hearts for a few minutes on all sides. Transfer to a plate.

Stir the flour into the pan. Add the meat or vegetable stock, marinade and tomato purée and leave to bubble for 5 minutes. Return the hearts to the pan. Cover and place in the pre-heated oven. Cook for 1 1/2 hours. Remove the hearts and keep warm.

Strain the sauce into a clean saucepan. Defat the sauce by laying sheets of kitchen paper over the top. Reduce if necessary.

Slice the hearts and arrange them in a pre-heated serving dish. Pour the sauce over. Serve immediately with mashed potatoes or creamed-spinach.

SERVES 6-8

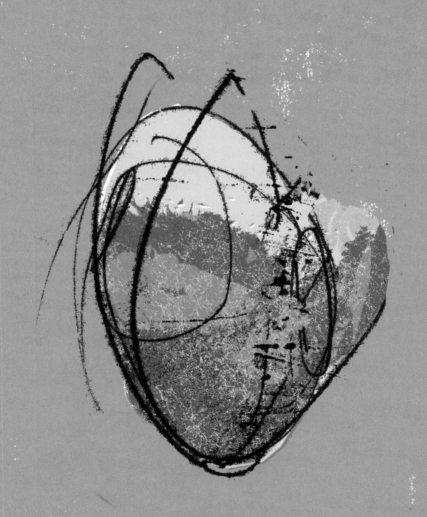

CALF'S HEART STEWED WITH PRUNES

COEUR DE VEAU EN COCOTTE
AUX PRUNEAUX

For this recipe, it is a good idea to ask your butcher to tie the heart for you as if it were a roast, unless you want to do it yourself.

2 tablespoons butter
12 baby onions, peeled
1 calf's heart, tied like a roast
1 tablespoon plain flour
200ml red wine
Sea salt and freshly ground pepper to taste
1 clove
1 sugar cube
12 dried prunes, soaked in warm water for 1 hour

Melt the butter in a large saucepan over a medium heat. Add the baby onions and sauté until lightly golden all over. Remove with a slotted spoon onto a plate. Set aside.

Add the heart to the pan and brown on all sides. Sprinkle with the flour and stir for a minute or so. Add the wine and 200ml water. Season with salt and pepper to taste. Add the clove and sugar cube. Bring to the boil and let it bubble for 3-4 minutes. Cover the pan, reduce the heat and simmer for 1½ hours. Turn the heart a couple of times during cooking and check the sauce to see that it does not dry out.

Twenty minutes before the heart is ready, return the onions to the pan. Drain the prunes and add to the pan. Simmer for another 20-30 minutes or until the onions are done and the sauce thickened. If the sauce is still quite thin at the end of cooking, remove the heart, onions and prunes onto a pre-heated serving platter and keep warm. Increase the heat and boil the sauce hard until it has reached the desired consistency. Pour the sauce over the meat and serve immediately.

SERVES 4

HAGGIS

Haggis is traditionally eaten at Hogmanay (New Year's Eve) and according to Theodora Fitzgibbon, author of *A Taste of Scotland*, the very best haggis is that made with deer's liver and not sheep's. The following recipe comes from F. Marian McNeill's *The Scot's Kitchen*. You could use bone marrow instead of suet, and if you do, you will need to double the cooking time.

1 sheep's pluck (heart, lungs and liver)
250g minced beef suet
2 medium onions, finely chopped
250g coarse oatmeal, toasted in a moderate oven
    for about 30 minutes
Good pinch cayenne pepper
$1/4$ teaspoon grated nutmeg
2 teaspoons dried herbs
Sea salt and freshly ground black pepper
1 large sheep's stomach, cleaned very well
300ml milk

Prepare the lungs as indicated on page 83 and discard the windpipe. Place in a large saucepan, together with the heart and liver. Cover with water and place over a medium heat. As the water comes to the boil, skim it clean and boil gently for $1^{1}/_{2}$ hours, or until completely tender. Remove the pluck from the pan. Trim away all gristle and nerves and chop them very fine. Strain and reserve the cooking liquid.

Put the chopped pluck in a large mixing bowl. Add the suet (or chopped bone marrow, if you are using it), chopped onions and toasted oatmeal. Add the cayenne pepper, nutmeg and dried herbs. Season with salt and pepper to taste. Mix well, adding enough of the pluck's cooking liquid to have a smooth mixture. The mixture should be highly seasoned.

Spoon the mixture into the sheep's stomach until it is three-quarters full. Sew the opening and place in a large pot. Cover with water. Add the milk. Place over a medium heat. As soon as the stomach swells up, prick it in several places, then reduce the heat and simmer for 3 hours, adding boiling water to cover if the water level goes below the stomach.
Serve very hot.

SERVES 8

PIG'S TROTTERS WITH PRUNES AND PINE NUTS

PEUS DE PORC AMB PRUNES I PINYONS

I lived in Barcelona for about 3 weeks in order to find and test some of the Spanish offal recipes for this book. At first, I shopped at the Boqueria. It was the only market I knew; also it was close to where I was staying. Then Margaret and Colin Visser introduced me to Mercat St Antoni, a gorgeous market off the tourist track and very close to their home. There they went to the most divinely gorgeous young charcutiers. Two young hunks whose mother, Señora Maria Font Llupia, gave me some wonderful recipes, one of which is this one below.

4 pig's trotters, preferably the front ones
   (manos in Spanish), cut in half lengthways
1 medium onion, studded with 2 cloves
1 medium leek, trimmed and washed
1 medium carrot
1 small parsnip
1 small branch celery, preferably with the leaves on
1 bouquet garni (thyme, laurel and parsley)

For the sofregit
6-7 tablespoons extra virgin olive oil
1 medium onion, very finely chopped
2-3 medium tomatoes, peeled, seeded and
   finely chopped
1 clove garlic, very finely chopped

To finish
20 prunes, preferably stoned
50g pine nuts
6 blanched almonds
1 small biscuit (Spanish galleta or digestive)

Put the pig's trotters in a large pot. Cover with water and place over a medium heat. Bring to the boil, then drain the trotters. Wipe the pot clean. Return the trotters to the pot and cover with fresh water. Add the vegetables and simmer, over a very low heat, for 3 hours, or until the trotters are done.

Make the sofregit: put the olive oil in a pan large enough to eventually take the cooked trotters and place over a medium heat. When the oil is hot, add the onions and cook, stirring occasionally, until golden. Add the garlic and when it has coloured, add the tomatoes. Simmer for 5-10 minutes, or until the excess liquid has evaporated and the sauce thickened. Set aside.

Let the trotters cool in the broth for a while, then remove onto a board. Carefully remove the bones, making sure you don't tear the meat. Strain the cooking broth and measure 600ml. Reserve the rest of the broth in case you need more.

Lay the pig's trotters in the sofregit. Carefully stir in the broth and simmer for 15 minutes. Add the prunes and pine nuts. Simmer for another 15 minutes.

Pound the almonds and biscuit in a mortar until you have a very fine paste. Add the mixture to the sauce about 2 or 3 minutes before the end of the cooking time. In Catalonia, this mixture is called picada and is used specifically to thicken sauces. Serve very hot with good bread.

SERVES 4

PIG'S TROTTERS IN MILK

MANOS DE CERDO CON LECHE

This recipe is a speciality of the Spanish region of Navarra. It's subtle sweet-savoury combination probably dates back to medieval times. The sauce can be used just as successfully with other white meats such as veal, chicken or even fish. In Pamplona it is used with salt cod. You can vary the recipe below by using cinnamon; boil the trotters in water only, then after frying them, stir a little flour into the oil before adding the same amount of milk, 1-2 tablespoons of sugar to taste, a cinnamon stick and a little stock. Finish as below. The end result will be quite different, intriguing and rather more refined.

2 salted pig's trotters, halved lengthways and soaked
    for 12 hours in a few changes of cold water

For the stock
1 medium onion, left whole
1 small carrot
1 small leek, trimmed and washed
1 small parsnip
1 branch celery with leaves on
1 bouquet garni (thyme and laurel)
Plain flour for dipping the trotters in

For the sauce
6-7 tablespoons extra virgin olive oil
1 small onion, finely chopped
1 clove garlic, finely chopped
1-2 sprigs parsley, most of the bottom stalk discarded,
    then finely chopped
4 tablespoons vegetable stock
200-250ml whole milk
3 tablespoons caster sugar

Drain the trotters and pat them dry. Singe over a gas flame and rinse under cold water. Place in a large pot.

Add the vegetables to the pot together with the bouquet garni. Cover well with water and place over a medium heat. As the water comes to the boil, skim it clean. Then lower the heat and simmer for $1\frac{1}{2}$-2 hours or until the trotters are done. Don't add any salt to the cooking broth. The trotters will still be slightly salted.

Lift the cooked trotters out of the stock with a slotted spoon. Carefully take the largest bone out of each half, pat them slightly dry, then dip them in flour and set aside.

Put the oil in a large sauté pan and place over a medium heat. When the oil is hot, fry the trotters on both sides until lightly golden. Transfer to a dish. Add the chopped onion to the oil and cook, stirring occasionally, until soft and transparent. Add the garlic and parsley and cook until the onion and garlic are golden and the parsley crisp.

Reduce the heat to low. Add the stock and let it bubble for a minute or so before adding the milk and sugar. When the milk starts bubbling, drop in the cooked trotters and simmer, covered, for 20-30 minutes or until the sauce has thickened and the meat is very hot. If you think that the sauce is not thick enough, stir in a little flour and simmer for 5 more minutes. Serve immediately.

SERVES 4 AS A STARTER
SERVES 2 AS A MAIN COURSE

BLANQUETTE OF SHEEP'S FEET

BLANQUETTE DE PIEDS DE MOUTON

The classic way to serve sheep's feet in France is with a sauce poulette but I prefer to serve them in a simplified blanquette sauce. You could vary the recipe by adding sautéed baby onions and mushrooms at the very end or even steamed fresh peas when in season.

8 sheep's feet, singed and washed well
Juice 1 lemon
1 onion studded with 3 cloves
1 carrot
1 branch celery with the leaves
1 leek, trimmed and washed
1 bouquet garni (thyme, laurel and parsley)
6 peppercorns
Sea salt

For the sauce
50g unsalted butter
50g plain flour
150ml cooking broth from the trotters
1 organic egg yolk
200ml crème fraîche
Juice of ½ lemon, or to taste
Sea salt and white pepper
A few sprigs flat-leaf parsley, most of the bottom stalk
   discarded, and finely chopped

Put the sheep's feet in a large saucepan and cover with water. Bring to the boil over a high heat. Drain the water off and then cover the feet with more fresh water. Add the lemon juice, vegetables, bouquet garni, pepper and salt to taste. Bring back to the boil, lower the heat and simmer for 1½ to 2 hours or until the feet are cooked.

Melt the butter in a saucepan, add the flour and stir for a minute or so. Slowly add the broth, stirring all the time, so as not to have lumps. Simmer for 5-10 minutes.

During that time beat the egg yolk into the cream and add the lemon juice. Add the cream mixture to the thickened broth and simmer for another couple of minutes, stirring continuously. Be careful not to let the sauce boil or it may curdle. Season with salt and pepper to taste.

Using a slotted spoon, lift the feet out of the cooking broth. Quickly remove the big bone out of each and arrange them on a pre-heated serving dish. Pour the sauce all over and sprinkle with the parsley. Serve immediately.

SERVES 4

CALF'S FEET

WITH CHICKPEAS AND WHEAT

HERGMA

I am not one for eating feet stew for breakfast. Raw liver perhaps, but not feet stew. Veal feet are, however, exactly what some Moroccans have for their breakfast. It is typical street fare, and the early morning sight of huge enamelware dishes filled with chickpeas and feet is common throughout Morocco. A friend of mine cooked her version of this classic street dish for me and it was quite exquisite. She sometimes uses sheep's feet instead of calf's. If you decide to follow her example, allow at least two sheep's feet per person.

250g chickpeas, soaked overnight with 1 teaspoon
   bicarbonate of soda
2 calf's feet singed, washed and cut across in half
   (ask your butcher to do this for you)
150g husked wheat
6 tablespoons extra virgin olive oil
4 garlic cloves
2 tablespoons ground cumin
2 tablespoons paprika
$\frac{1}{4}$ teaspoon crushed chillies
Sea salt

Place the calf's feet in a large pot. Be sure to wash them really well otherwise they are liable to retain a slightly unfresh taste. Add $3\frac{1}{2}$ litres of water and place over a medium-high heat. Bring to the boil, then cover the pan and cook for 45 minutes.

Add the chickpeas, wheat, garlic and spices and boil for another $1\frac{1}{2}$ hours, or until very tender.

By this time the cooking broth should have reduced to an unctuous sauce. If it hasn't, increase the heat to high and boil hard until it is the right consistency. Add sea salt to taste. Serve very hot.

SERVES 4-6

CALF'S KIDNEYS
SAUCE ROBERT

ROGNONS DE VEAU SAUCE ROBERT

When cooking calf's kidneys some recipes tell you to leave a little of the fat over the kidney- no easy job. After many failed attempts, I now ask my butcher to trim the kidneys for me, including the complete removal of the core.

75g unsalted butter
Sea salt and freshly ground pepper
2 calf's kidneys (about 500g)

For the sauce
100ml white wine
½ tablespoon Dijon mustard
A few sprigs parsley, most of the bottom stalks
    removed, and finely chopped
Juice of ¼ lemon, or to taste

Put 50g of butter in a saucepan large enough to take the 2 kidneys and place over a medium heat. When the butter is very hot but not burning, add the kidneys. Season with salt and pepper to taste and cook for 4-6 minutes on each side, depending on how pink you like your kidneys.

When the kidneys are done, remove them onto a plate and keep warm. Pour the white wine into the pan to deglaze and boil hard until the wine is reduced. Take the pan off the heat and stir in the mustard, parsley and lemon juice. Add the rest of the butter, cut into small pieces, and stir until melted.

Quickly cut the kidneys in half lengthways and return to the pan with their juices. Stir the juices into the sauce and serve immediately in a pre-heated serving dish with boiled new potatoes.

SERVES 4

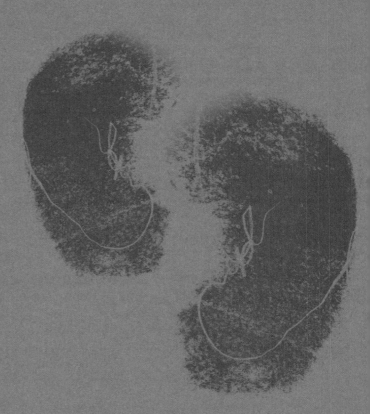

LAMB'S KIDNEYS BAKED INSIDE POTATOES

I first found this brilliant way of preparing kidneys in Ambrose Heath's classic book, *Meat*, published in 1971. I was immediately intrigued by the concept but wondered if the kidneys would still be good after so long in the oven – it takes at least 1½ hours to bake a large potato! So I approached Heath's recipe with some scepticism. However, on cutting open the potato and biting into the kidney, I was staggered to discover that it had remained moist, tender and succulent. Amazing! It must, I suppose, be due to the fact that the kidneys cook so slowly and gently, nestled and protected inside the potatoes. The potatoes too were absolutely wonderful, soaked through with kidney juices and slightly spicy from the pepper.

6 large baking potatoes, washed and dried
6 lamb's kidneys, stripped of their fat and the
   cores removed
Sea salt and freshly ground black pepper

Pre-heat the oven to 180°C/350°F/Gas 4.

Cut off one third of each potato horizontally, choosing the knobbly side for the top third – this will eventually be a lid to cover the kidney with; the flatter bottom part will make it easier for the potatoes to sit straight on the baking sheet.

Using a grapefruit knife, core out enough of the inside of the larger part of the potato to create a snug nest for the lamb's kidney. Salt and pepper the inside of the cavity to taste, and place the kidney inside it. Salt and pepper the kidney.

Remove a little from the inside of the potato lid so that it sits flush on the bottom part. Salt and pepper its inside to taste and place it over the kidney to cover. The potato should look as if it still whole. Prepare and fill the remaining potatoes in the same way.

Place the potatoes on a baking sheet, leaving a little space between each. Bake in the pre-heated oven for 1½ to 2 hours, or until the potatoes are completely done. You can test for doneness by squeezing the potato to see if it gives. Serve immediately with the herb butter on page 128 and a green vegetable, such as creamed spinach or steamed broccoli.

SERVES 6

KIDNEY STEW WITH PEAS

RIÑONES CON GUISANTES

Another recipe from Senoza Ilupia and a very nice and rather refreshing way of preparing kidneys. As always, take special care not to overcook the kidney.

2 calf's kidneys (about 500g), cut into
    bite-sized chunks
Sea salt
Juice of 1 lemon
100g lard
1 medium onion, finely chopped
2 garlic cloves, finely chopped
A few sprigs of flat-leaf parsley, leaves only,
    finely chopped
Scant tablespoon plain flour
100ml dry sherry
1 x 400g Italian tin tomatoes, chopped small
Pepper to taste
500g fresh garden peas, or equivalent frozen

Put the kidney pieces in a large bowl and season with a little salt. Add the lemon juice. Stir, then cover with a clean kitchen cloth and set aside.

Melt half the lard in a saucepan large enough to eventually take the kidneys and peas, and place over a medium heat. Add the chopped onion and cook until soft and transparent. Add the garlic and parsley and carry on cooking until the onion and garlic turn golden and the parsley is crisp.

Stir in the flour, then the sherry and tomatoes and season with salt and pepper to taste. Simmer for 20 minutes.

Put the remaining lard in a frying pan and place over a medium-high heat. When the lard is really hot, sauté the kidneys for a minute or two, until browned on all sides. Transfer the kidneys with a slotted spoon to the tomato sauce. Sauté the peas in the same fat. Remove with a slotted spoon and add to the kidneys. Simmer for 10 more minutes or until both meat and peas are done to your liking. Taste, and adjust the seasoning if necessary. Serve very hot with plain rice.

KIDNEYS COOKED IN SHERRY

RINONES AL XERES

You could also use pig's or calf's kidneys in this lovely Spanish classic. Whichever kidney you eventually use though, the most important thing to remember is not to overcook them, as they will then become tough and rubbery.

750g lamb's kidneys, core discarded, cubed
  and soaked in water with a little lemon juice
4 tablespoons extra virgin olive oil
1 small onion, very finely chopped
1 garlic clove, very finely chopped
1 tablespoon plain flour
120ml dry sherry
100ml beef stock
1 bay leaf
Sea salt and freshly ground black pepper
2 tablespoons finely chopped flat-leaf parsley

Drain the kidneys and pat dry with kitchen paper.

Put the olive oil and onions in a sauté pan and place over a low heat. Cook, stirring occasionally until lightly golden. Add the kidneys and garlic and cook for 2-3 minutes, turning the meat regularly to brown them all over.

Stir in the flour. Add the sherry, stock and bay leaf. Season with salt and pepper to taste and simmer for 15 minutes – be sure not to let the sauce boil. The sauce should thicken and become velvety. Transfer to a pre-heated serving dish. Sprinkle with the chopped parsley and serve immediately with plain rice.

SERVES 4

LITTLE POTS OF CURRIED KIDNEYS

This is an appealing and unusual way of preparing and serving kidneys. An excellent dinner party dish.

Breadcrumbs
Unsalted butter, for frying
1 onion, finely chopped
2 teaspoons mild curry paste
6 lamb's kidneys, sliced in half, core removed,
  then cut in small chunks
275ml double cream

Fry the breadcrumbs in butter until they begin to crisp. Let cool.

In another pan, sauté the onion in 1 tablespoon butter until softened. Add the curry paste and cook gently for 2 more minutes. Transfer to a bowl and set aside.

Add more butter to the pan and quickly sauté the pieces of kidney until sealed. Remove with a slotted spoon and mix with the curried onion.

Pre-heat the oven to 220°C/425°F/Gas 7.

Place equal quantities of kidneys and onion in four 150ml pots. Add a quarter of the cream to each pot. They should be two-thirds full. Stir well.

Put the pots on a tray and place in the pre-heated oven for about 5 minutes, or until the sauce begins to bubble. Stir again and sprinkle a good layer of breadcrumbs over the top of each. Cook until the tops are golden brown and the sauce is bubbling. The result should be lightly cooked kidneys in a creamy curried sauce with a crisp topping. Serve immediately with a green salad of steamed green beans.

SERVES 4

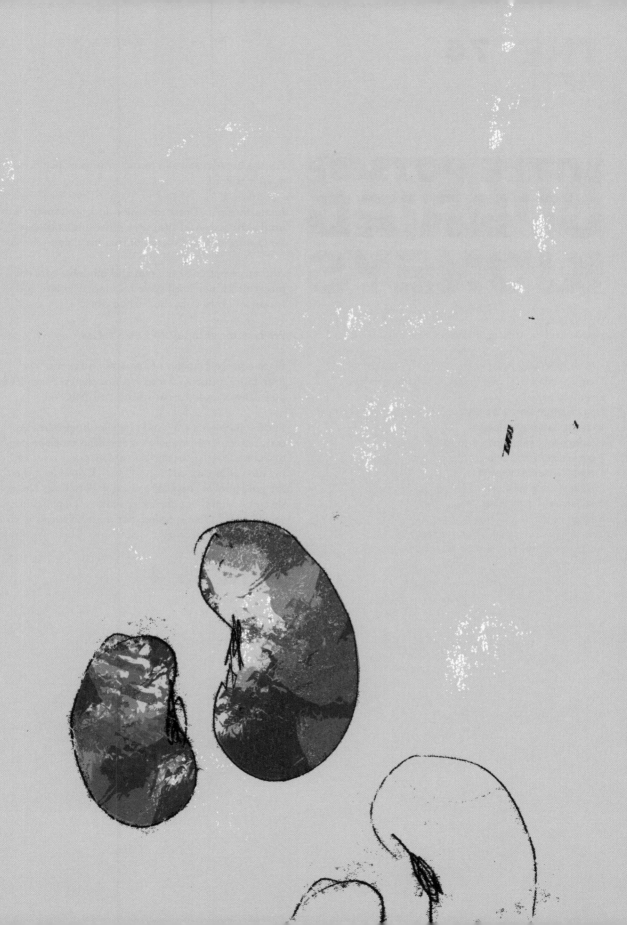

KIDNEYS
AND SNOW PEAS

YAOZ CHAO XUEDOU

A classic Chinese recipe for pork kidneys that is both wonderfully simple and perfectly delicious.

4 pork kidneys
2 spring onions, sliced in 8cm sections and finely shredded
1½cm piece fresh ginger, peeled and finely shredded
½ teaspoon caster sugar
½ teaspoon salt, plus extra for stir-frying
1 tablespoon cornflour
1 teaspoon sesame oil
3 tablespoons soy sauce
1 tablespoon rice wine
Peanut oil for stir-frying
200g fresh snow peas, trimmed and washed
¼ cup dried tree ears, soaked for 20 minutes in 250ml hot water

Rinse the kidneys and cut each horizontally, into 3 or 4 slices. Discard the core part and lightly score one side of each piece in small diamond shapes. Slice each piece into 1½cm wide slivers. Rinse again under cold water and drain off all excess moisture. Place in a bowl.

Add the spring onion, ginger, sugar, salt, cornflour, sesame oil, soy sauce and rice wine. Mix well.

Place a wok over a high heat for 15 seconds. Add 2 tablespoons of peanut oil. When the oil starts smoking, add the snow peas and stir-fry for 30 seconds. Season with ½ teaspoon salt and fry for another 45 seconds, then add 1 tablespoon water. Stir-fry for 30 seconds. Remove onto a serving dish.

Return the wok to the heat and add 4 tablespoons of peanut oil. When the oil is hot, add the tree ears and ¼ teaspoon salt. Stir-fry for 15 seconds.

Add the kidneys and their marinade and stir-fry for 30 seconds. Return the snow peas to the wok and stir-fry for 2 more minutes. Serve immediately with plain rice.

SERVES 4

STEAK & KIDNEY
PUDDING

Even though I arrived in England over 30 years ago, there are still certain dishes that I am not overly familiar with, nor, to be truthful, very keen on; one such is steak and kidney pie or pudding. The difference between the pie and the pudding is both in the pastry and method of cooking. The meat mixture remains the same, but is completely encased in a pastry made with suet for the pudding, while it is just covered with a shortcrust pastry for the pie. The pudding is then steamed while the pie is baked. The following recipe is for a pie and comes from one of Britain's most famous pubs, the Nobody Inn, in Devon, and is taken from the groundbreaking book on gastropub cooking, *Real Pub Food*.

For the filling
1 medium onion, finely chopped
2-3 tablespoons sunflower oil
1kg braising steak, diced into cubes
500g calf's kidneys, core removed and diced
   into cubes
200ml bitter beer
200ml organic vegetable stock
Sea salt and freshly ground black pepper

For the pastry
175g fresh breadcrumbs
75g plain flour
50g suet
1 organic egg, beaten

Put the onion and oil in a large pot and place over a medium heat. Fry the onion until lightly golden.

Add the meat and cook for 2-3 minutes, stirring occasionally, until browned all over. Add the beer and vegetable stock. Season with salt and pepper to taste and lower the heat. Cover and simmer for about 3 hours, or until the meat is very tender.

One and a half hours before the meat is ready, make the pastry. Mix all the ingredients for the pastry with $1\frac{1}{2}$ tablespoons water and knead until you have an homogeneous dough. Cover and let rest for 1 hour.

Transfer the meat with a slotted spoon to a large bowl. Let cool. Reserve the cooking broth.

Roll out two thirds of the dough to a disk large enough to line a pudding basin. Line the basin with the rolled out pastry, letting the excess dough hang over the edges. Spoon the meat into the pastry. Roll out the remaining piece of pastry to a disk large enough to cover the top of the basin. Place over the filling and seal the edges. Trim off any excess pastry. Cover with a pleated piece of greaseproof paper and steam for 45 minutes.

During this time, reduce the cooking broth until you have a thick sauce.

Carefully invert the pudding onto a serving platter. Pour a little sauce all over it. Serve immediately with the remaining sauce and boiled new potatoes.

SERVES 6

BRAISED CALF'S LIVER

FOIE DE VEAU BRAISÉ

The following classic way to serve liver is, sadly, not so common any longer, even though the preparation is fairly simple. You will need to lard the liver and this can be easily done by your butcher. Larding meat means simply threading pieces of pig's backfat (lard in French) into the meat, so that some of the fat melts inside it during cooking to keep it moist. If you are feeling particularly adept and have a larding needle to hand you could have a go at doing it yourself. There are a number of different ways of larding meat but here the strips of fat need to be threaded symmetrically and in well-spaced lines across the liver, so that when you slice the liver to serve it, you have little cubes of lard running along the middle of each slice.

1.25kg calf's liver in one piece
150g pork fat (lard), cut into strips about 1cm thick
    and the same width as your piece of liver
Sea salt and freshly ground black pepper

For the marinade
1 large onion, thinly sliced
6 sprigs flat-leaf parsley
2 sprigs thyme
1 bay leaf
200ml white wine
2 tablespoons extra virgin olive oil

To finish
Piece of fresh caul large enough to wrap the liver
30g unsalted butter
2 teaspoons plain flour
200ml veal or vegetable stock
1 tablespoon tomato purée

Ask your butcher to lard the liver or do it yourself. Either way, it is a good idea to season the strips of pork fat with a little salt and pepper before larding.

Mix the ingredients for the marinade in a large bowl. Season with salt and pepper to taste and add the liver. Scoop over some of the marinade ingredients to cover the top of the liver. Let marinate for 2 hours, turning the liver at regular intervals.

Pre-heat your oven to 150°C/300°F/Gas 2.

Take the liver out of the marinade – reserve the marinade – and wipe it dry. Wrap it in the caul and tie loosely with thread, as you would do a roast.

Put the butter in a large braising pan that can fit into the oven and place over a medium-high heat. Brown the liver for 2 minutes on each side. Reduce the heat to moderate and continue browning the liver for another 8 minutes, turning it regularly. Do not cover the pan during this time.

Transfer the liver to a plate and stir the flour into the butter. Add the stock, marinade and tomato purée. Bring to the boil, stirring continuously. Season with a little more pepper. Return the liver to the pan. Cover and braise in the pre-heated oven for 45 minutes.

Remove the liver onto a serving platter and let it rest while you defat the sauce, reducing it if necessary. Taste and adjust the seasoning, if necessary. Untie the liver and either slice it before serving or serve it whole. In either case, strain the sauce over the meat and serve very hot with green beans or baby carrots and boiled new potatoes. Or serve warm with a salad, either with the re-heated sauce or without.

SERVES 4-6

LIVER
WITH SNOW PEAS

ZHUGAN CHAO XUEDOU

This is a recipe from the Chinese cookery writer, Mrs Chiang, all of whose recipes are not only delicious but fairly quick to cook – once you have shopped for the unusual ingredients and done all the necessary preparation, that is. I remember my visit to Singapore, many years ago, to stay with my great, and sadly late friend, Don Munson. He had a housekeeper who was also the cook, and a wonderful one at that. I always went shopping with her in the early mornings. I would then spend the rest of the morning watching her cook. I was consistently amazed at how long it took her to prepare a dish that then cooked in just 2-3 minutes.

¼ cup dried tree ears
450g pig's or calf's liver, sliced across into very
   thin slices
1 spring onion, cut in 5cm sections, then finely
   shredded
3 tablespoons soy sauce
1½ teaspoons sesame oil
1 tablespoon Chinese rice wine
½ teaspoon caster sugar
1 tablespoon cornflour
120g snow peas, trimmed and washed
3 fresh water chestnuts, peeled and thinly sliced
1 small carrot, thinly sliced
Peanut oil for stir-frying
Fine sea salt
1 tablespoon hot chilli paste
2½cm piece fresh ginger, peeled and cut into
   julienne strips

Put the tree ears to soak in 500ml boiling water.

Put the liver in a large bowl. Add the onion, soy sauce, sesame oil, rice wine, sugar and cornflour. Mix well. Let marinate for 30 minutes.

Heat a wok over a high flame for 15 seconds. Add 1 tablespoon of peanut oil. When the oil starts smoking, stir-fry the snow peas for about 45 seconds.

Add the water chestnuts and carrots and stir-fry for another 30 seconds. Add 1 teaspoon salt and the drained tree ears and stir-fry for another 30 seconds before adding 4 tablespoons of water. Cook the vegetables for another 20 seconds, then remove onto a plate.

Wipe the wok clean with kitchen paper and return to the heat. When the wok is hot, add 5 tablespoons of peanut oil. Add 2 tablespoons of water to the liver. When the oil starts smoking, add the chilli paste and julienned ginger. Stir-fry for a few seconds then add the liver and stir-fry for 1 minute. Return the vegetables to the wok and stir-fry for 1½ minutes. Serve immediately with plain rice.

SERVES 4

CALF'S LIVER
AND RED ONIONS

Here is a simple, hearty way to prepare liver that may take a long time to cook, but will hardly take any time to prepare.

4 tablespoons extra virgin olive oil
30g unsalted butter
450g red onions, thinly sliced
1 teaspoon fresh thyme leaves
1 tablespoon lemon juice
Sea salt
Freshly ground black pepper
8 x 65g thin slices of calf's liver
Few sprigs flat-leaf parsley, most of the stalks
   discarded, then finely chopped

Put half the oil and half the butter in a large frying pan and place over a very low heat. Add the onion and thyme and cook, stirring occasionally, for 1 hour, or until shiny and soft. Add the lemon juice and season with salt and pepper to taste.

Heat the remaining oil and butter in another frying pan over a medium-high heat. Season the liver slices with salt and pepper to taste and fry for 1 minute on each side until golden brown on the outside but still pink on the inside.

Transfer the liver to a large pre-heated serving platter. Spoon the red onions all over. Garnish with the chopped parsley and serve immediately.

SERVES 4

CALF'S LIVER WITH LEMON

FEGATO DI VITELLO AL LIMONE

My two great friends in Italy, Ilaria Borletti and Suni Agnelli, decided not so long ago to give me a flat for a month as a present to try out life in Rome. The flat was inside a lovely palazzo just by the old Jewish ghetto. Well, life turned out to be so enchanting that I ended up doing very little work. Instead, I spent my time enjoying the sights, the seaside at weekends and, of course, the food. I am not sure if the following recipe is a Roman speciality but I had it in my local restaurant in Piazza Margana a couple of times and it is a gorgeous way of cooking liver. Also it just takes minutes to prepare.

2 slices calf's liver, about 1cm thick
Plain flour seasoned with sea salt and freshly ground
   black pepper to taste
50g butter
1 lemon, sliced very thinly
Juice of 1/2 lemon
1 tablespoon chopped parsley

Dip the liver in the seasoned flour and shake well.

Put the butter in a large frying pan and place over a medium-high heat. When the butter is really hot, fry the liver for 1-2 minutes on each side, or until done to your liking. Remove onto a serving platter and keep warm.

Quickly sauté the lemon slices in the pan until crisp and arrange over the liver. Deglaze the pan with the lemon juice and pour the sauce over the meat. Garnish with the chopped parsley. Serve immediately with sautéed spinach.

SERVES 2

FAGGOTS

FFAGODAU

A faggot means a bundle, and this is exactly what
faggots are, a bundle of minced liver and onions
wrapped in caul and either baked or stewed.
Some recipes tell you to cook the liver and onion first,
others tell you to use them raw. I prefer to use them
raw. This means that the faggots will remain moist.
You can also stew faggots in a rich brown sauce
instead of plainly baking them.

450g pig's liver
2 medium onions, quartered
100g breadcrumbs
75g suet
2 tablespoons chopped sage
Sea salt and freshly ground black pepper
Large piece of fresh caul, cut into 8 pieces large
    enough to wrap the faggots
A little lard to grease the baking dish

Put the liver and onions in a food processor and
process until coarsely chopped. Transfer to a mixing
bowl.

Add the breadcrumbs, chopped suet and sage.
Season with salt and pepper to taste.

Shape the mixture into 8 balls and wrap each in caul.

Pre-heat the oven to 180°C/350°F/Gas 4. Grease a
baking dish with a little lard.

Place the faggots in the greased baking dish and bake
for about 30 minutes

Remove the faggots and keep warm. Deglaze the dish
with a little boiling water and stir in a little flour to
make a gravy. Serve very hot with mashed potatoes or
let cool until they are room temperature and serve
with a green salad.

SERVES 4

SHEEP'S LUNGS
IN TOMATO SAUCE

JAKHNET FISHEH

Of all offal, lungs are perhaps the least interesting gastronomically. Even so, I used to love them when I lived in Beirut many years ago. But the last time I was there and my mother prepared them for me, I was rather less enthusiastic. They seemed to taste rather bland and the texture wasn't as pleasing as I had remembered. I wonder if new farming methods have affected both taste and texture. Still, they make a pretty cheap and good stew, especially if you get them from a reliable butcher. Lungs are also pretty good simply seasoned with salt and pepper and grilled over a charcoal fire.

1 pair of sheep's lungs
1 cinnamon stick
Sea salt

For the tomato sauce
60g unsalted butter
2 medium onions, thinly sliced
3 x 400g tins Italian tomatoes, finely chopped
1/4 teaspoon finely ground black pepper
1/4 teaspoon seven-pepper mixture (or ground allspice)
Scant 1/4 teaspoon ground cinnamon

Rinse the lungs well under cold water. Put in a saucepan and cover with water. Add the cinnamon stick and salt to taste and place over a medium-high heat. As the water comes to the boil, skim it clean. Then cover and cook for 40-45 minutes, or until the meat is done. You will notice the colour changing from a fresh pink to a rather off-putting grey. Don't let that discourage you, the colour will not matter once the meat is submerged in the tomato sauce.

Melt the butter in a saucepan and sauté the onions until lightly golden. Add the chopped tomatoes and seasonings and simmer for 5 minutes. When the lungs are done, cut them up in bite-sized pieces and add to the sauce. Simmer for 25-30 minutes, or until the sauce has thickened. Serve hot with plain rice or good bread.

SERVES 4-6

PIG'S LUNGS
WITH ALMOND JUICE

This is an extremely unusual recipe from the book *Cooking with Honk Kong's Top Chefs*. Pig's lungs are rarely seen for sale outside China, though I'm sure that a willing butcher or farm shop outlet would be able to supply a keen offal cook in search of excitement and a way to surprise his/her guests.

150g regular almonds
10g bitter almonds
2 pig's lungs
300g lean pork
70g cooked ham
Fine sea salt

Soak half the almonds and ¾ of the bitter ones in 200ml water for 1 hour. Put the almonds and their soaking water in a blender and process until finely ground. Drain the almond juice through a very fine sieve and press on the pulp to extract as much liquid as you can.

Fill the lungs with water and rinse until there is no more trace of blood and the lungs have turned white.

Put the lungs in a saucepan. Add 2½ litres water and place over a medium heat. Bring to a boil, then lower the heat and simmer for 10 minutes. Drain the lungs, rinse and place in a big clay container. Add 1½ litres water, the remaining almonds, the pork and ham and steam for 3 hours.

Add the almond juice and steam for another 10 minutes. Add salt to taste and serve immediately with plain rice.

SERVES 4

CALF'S SWEETBREADS WITH GIROLLES

RIS DE VEAU AU GIROLLES

The finest sweetbreads are those that come from milk-fed calves. During one of my recipe-testing stays in Paris – in a flat kindly lent to me by Philip and Mary Hyman, the great experts on French food and cooking – I used an excellent butcher in Montmartre who provided me with some of the best sweetbreads I have ever had. The pommes (sweetbreads from around the heart) were a perfect shape. Even the longer ones from around the neck had a good shape – they can sometimes be quite straggly. The colour was a delicate pink with hardly any blood, which meant I did not need to soak them. In fact, Mr. Christian Valadou at Boucherie Ruffet, who gave me the following recipe, told me that I never needed to soak sweetbreads, especially not those from milk-fed calves. This would only take away from their delicate taste, he said.
If you can't find girolles, use another fresh and tasty mushroom or use 50g dried morels, which you will need to soak beforehand.

1 pair of calf's sweetbreads from around the heart,
   weighing about 500g, trimmed and cut into
   2 escalopes, each about 1½cm thick
Plain flour, seasoned with sea salt and freshly ground
   black pepper
100g girolles
60g unsalted butter
1 tablespoon Cognac
2 tablespoons crème fraîche

Soak the sweetbreads if they are bloody and pat them dry before using.

Roll the sweetbreads in a little flour. Shake well and set aside.

Rinse the mushrooms under cold water, dry them with a clean kitchen cloth and cut in half lengthways.

Melt half the butter in a frying pan over a medium heat. When the butter is hot, add the sweetbreads and cook for 3 minutes on each side. Set aside.

Melt the rest of the butter in another frying pan over a medium-high heat. When the butter is hot, sauté the mushrooms for about 3 minutes. Add the Cognac and let it bubble for a few seconds. Add the cream and let it bubble for a minute or two, or until the sauce is thickened. Season with salt and pepper to taste.

Using a slotted spoon, transfer the cooked sweetbreads to the mushroom sauce and turn them to coat all over. Serve immediately with a baguette to mop up the sauce and a vegetable of your choice.

SERVES 2

CALF'S SWEETBREADS WITH CAPERS

This is a simple and delectable way to serve calf's sweetbreads and comes from Keith Floyd's very first book, *Floyd's Food*, published some years before he rose to stardom.

750g calf's sweetbreads
Plain flour
100g unsalted butter
1 tablespoon capers
Few sprigs flat-leaf parsley, bottom stalk discarded,
    then finely chopped
Pinch grated nutmeg
Sea salt and freshly ground black pepper
4 lemon halves

Put the sweetbreads in a bowl and leave under slowly running cold water. Let the water run until all traces of blood have been washed away. Blanch the sweetbreads and let cool.

Peel off as much of the outer skin as you can without tearing into the sweetbreads and press under a weighted plate for an hour or so. Slice the sweetbreads into 5cm scallops. Carefully pat dry with kitchen paper and lightly sprinkle with flour.

Melt half the butter in a large frying pan over a medium-high heat. When the butter is hot, fry the sweetbreads until golden all over, about 2 minutes on each side. Remove onto a plate, leaving all the burned bits behind.

Melt the remaining butter in a clean pan until it foams and turns brown. Add the sweetbreads together with the capers and nutmeg. Season with salt and pepper and swish quickly around the pan. Serve immediately on warmed plates with the lemon halves and a green salad.

SERVES 4

CASSEROLE OF CALF'S SWEETBREADS AND LAMB'S FEET

A classic French casserole dish from the great chef Pierre Orsiat of the Restaurant Pierre Orsiat in Lyon.

50g red pepper, cut into small dice
50g green pepper, cut into small dice
50g celery root, cut into small dice
4 cooked lamb's feet, halved lengthways and bones taken out
1/2 cooked calf's foot, then meat taken off the bone and diced
Thyme
Bay leaf
3 tablespoons white wine
1 1/2 tablespoons wine vinegar
1/2 organic chicken bouillon cube
1 shallot, finely chopped
250ml light veal stock
200g calf's sweetbreads, diced and sautéed in butter
1/2 large tablespoonful Dijon mustard
Sea salt and freshly ground black pepper
Chopped chives for garnish

Blanch the peppers and celery root. Refresh, drain and set aside.

Put the lamb's feet and diced calf's foot in a saucepan with the thyme and bay leaf, half the white wine and the vinegar. Half cover with water and add the chicken bouillon cube. Simmer for 15 minutes. Strain the meat and keep covered. Reserve the cooking liquid.

Reduce the remaining white wine by $^4/_5$ in a cast iron pot. Add the chopped shallots, the veal stock and the feet's cooking liquid. Simmer gently for a few minutes.

Add the blanched diced peppers and celery root. Then add the sweetbreads and lamb and calf's feet. Simmer for 15 minutes.

Just before you are ready to serve, stir in the mustard, making sure you do not break up the lamb's feet. Season with salt and pepper, to taste. Serve in deep plates that you will have heated. Garnish with chives and serve with spoons.

SERVES 4

FRICASSEE OF SWEETBREADS WITH KIDNEYS

FRICASSÉE DE RIS AUX ROGNONS

A delicious and simple way to combine sweetbreads with kidneys.

1 pair fresh calf's sweetbreads from around the heart
1 calf's kidney
50g clarified butter
Plain flour, seasoned with sea salt and freshly ground
   black pepper
2 shallots, finely chopped
2 tablespoons Cognac
50-75ml white veal stock
75g fresh white mushrooms, thinly sliced
50-75ml double cream

Prepare and blanch the sweetbreads as indicated in the recipe on p87.

Skin and cut out the core of the kidney. Separate into individual nodes.

Heat the clarified butter in a sauté pan over a medium high heat. Cook the kidneys quickly on both sides until firmed up but still pink inside. Remove and keep warm.

Dust the sweetbreads with seasoned flour and sauté gently until golden. Transfer to a dish and keep warm.

Sauté the shallots in the juices in the pan and deglaze with Cognac. Add the veal stock and mushrooms and reduce. Add the double cream and boil until the sauce has thickened. Season with salt and pepper to taste.

Return the kidneys and sweetbreads to the sauce and simmer until the meat has re-heated. Season with salt and pepper to taste. Serve with saffron rice and petits pois.

SERVES 4

ANDOUILLETTES AU FOUR

The most famous and, reputedly the best andouillettes, come from Troyes, where they are still made by hand. The dressed meats – all pork, two thirds intestines to one third stomach – are coiled and then encased into the large intestine with the help of a wooden spatula and a thread. This process is known as 'tirée à la ficelle' (pulled with a thread). Whenever you read this description, or simply ficelle, on a restaurant menu, you will know that the andouillete is hand-made. Another label that signals quality is A.A.A.A. which stands for the Association Amicale des Amateurs d'Authentiques Andouillettes, a gastronomic society that upholds the authentic tradition of andouillete. There are many regional variations on andouillete; in Lyons, for instance, they use fraise de veau (veal intestinal membrane) instead of pork intestines. Andouillettes, traditionally, are pre-cooked in broth or milk, and usually sold coated in aspic jelly or breadcrumbs. All you have to do then is grill or fry them. Alternatively, you can go for the slightly more elaborate preparation below, which I serve with a celeriac or potato purée. You could also serve andouillettes on a bed of choucroute as they do in Strasbourg.

50g unsalted butter
12 shallots, very finely chopped
4 andouillettes
200ml white wine
Sea salt and freshly ground black pepper to taste

Pre-heat the oven to 180°C/350°F/Gas 4.

Put the butter in a medium-sized oven-to-table dish and melt over a a medium heat. Add the shallots and cook until soft and translucent.

Make 3 or 4 diagonal incisions into the skin of each andouillette to stop them from bursting and fry with the shallots until lightly golden. Add the white wine and transfer the dish to the pre-heated oven. Bake for 20 minutes, turning them over half-way through. Serve very hot.

SERVES 4

BLACK PUDDING

BOUDIN NOIR

Boudin or black pudding is one of the oldest and most revered of cooked 'meats', and is made all over Europe. Made with pig's blood and fat, the mixture is then seasoned with spices and herbs and funnelled into an intestine casing. It is then cooked very gently in a broth. There are endless variations: with added onions in Paris, chestnuts in Auvergne, rice in Spain or oats in Scotland, to name but a few. Boudin is sold in individual pre-sealed pieces or cut from a length to be fried or grilled and served with apples or potatoes. There are some that are eaten cold, such as the Catalan butifarra. The Norwegian blood sausage looks like a black salami and is eaten as such. The following recipe was given to me by Paul Hughes, master charcutier at the Ginger Pig in London's wonderful Borough Market.

Lard
700g pork backfat, diced small
500g cooked head meat and ears, diced small
$\frac{1}{2}$ bunch marjoram, leaves only
400g leeks, trimmed, cleaned and finely chopped
75g garlic
2 tablespoons sea salt
1 tablespoon freshly ground black pepper
2 teaspoons ground allspice
250g breadcrumbs
250ml full-fat organic milk
1 litre pig's blood
Ox intestines, stripped of their fat and cleaned very well

Put a little lard in a large heavy-bottomed pot and place over a medium heat. Add the diced backfat and stir until translucent. Add the head meats, marjoram, leeks, garlic and seasonings and stir for a few minutes.

Mix the breadcrumbs and milk together and add to the meats, stirring all the time.

Finally, add the blood and stir until all the ingredients are suspended in the blood. Remove from the heat and, using a funnel, fill the intestines, with the mixture. Tie the ends then tie the sausage into a ring.

Fill a large pot with water and bring the water to a boil. Reduce the heat to low and wait until the water is barely simmering before adding the boudin. As soon as the boudin starts swelling, prick it in a few places so that it doesn't burst. Gently simmer for about 20 minutes, then take out of the pan and let cool. You can keep this boudin for at least a week in the refrigerator before cooking it, simply fried in a little butter. Serve with apple purée and sautéed potatoes.

SERVES 8-10

OX TRIPE
ANDALUCIAN STYLE

CALLOS A LA ANDALUZA

My first ever visit to Spain, more than 20 years ago, was to Marbella, which by then had lost some of its shine as a jet-setting play-ground for the rich and famous. However, the place had, and still has, great restaurants, as well as a fabulous food market and wonderful tapas bars, including one in the market itself, where we would regularly stop for a hearty late breakfast. Our choice always included caracoles (snails) and the following recipe for tripe. You may find that it is bit too much for breakfast, but do try it for lunch or supper as it is really quite delicious.

150g chickpeas, soaked overnight with ½ teaspoon of bicarbonate of soda
4 pimentos choriceros (dried sweet red peppers)
1 cominos
50g unsalted butter
2 tablespoons extra virgin olive oil
1 slice bread
1 medium onion, finely chopped
2 garlic cloves, finely chopped
2 tablespoons finely chopped flat-leaf parsley
1 rioja chorizo (small and mild), sliced medium-thin

2 medium tomatoes, peeled, seeded and finely chopped
1 walnut
1 clove
Sea salt and freshly ground black pepper
200ml of white wine
500g cooked ox tripe, cut into bite-sized pieces

Rinse the chickpeas well. Drain and put in a saucepan. Cover with water and bring to the boil over a medium heat. Lower the heat and simmer for 1 hour, or until they are tender but not mushy.

Put the dried peppers and cominos to soak separately in warm water.

Heat the butter and oil in a saucepan. First fry the bread until crisp and golden on both sides and remove onto kitchen paper. Fry the onion until soft and transparent. Add the garlic and parsley and continue frying until crisp and golden. Add the chorizo slices and sauté for a couple of minutes before adding the chopped tomatoes. Cook until the excess liquid has evaporated.

While the sauce is cooking, put the walnut, fried bread, clove and a little salt and pepper in a mortar and crush with a pestle until very fine. Set aside.

Drain the peppers and cut them open. Discard the seeds and scrape the flesh out with a knife. Add to the sauce together with the white wine and salt to taste. Then add the tripe and the cooked and drained chickpeas. Cover with water or broth and simmer gently for 1 hour or so.

Stir in the walnut and bread mixture and let bubble for a few more minutes until the sauce thickens. Taste and adjust the seasoning, if necessary. Serve very hot.

SERVES 4

CURRIED TRIPE

PENSLAWER

Here is an unusual way of preparing tripe that comes from the late Sonia Allison's delightful book on the food of the Cape Malay community in South Africa, *Cooking Cape Malay*. Allison says in her introduction to the recipe, 'Sunday Happiness after prayers at the mosque is to come home to penslawer, the Cape Malay answer to British tripe and onions. If you like tripe, which some of us do, this is a magnificent piece of culinary engineering, not to be missed even if it means hunting around for the tripe.'

1.5kg dressed tripe, washed very well
2 teaspoons sea salt
2 tablespoons sunflower oil
2 large onions, finely chopped
2 garlic cloves, finely chopped
2½cm piece of ginger, peeled and finely chopped
1 teaspoon ground turmeric
1 tablespoon mild korma curry powder
1 teaspoon ground coriander
2 teaspoons ground cumin
2 teaspoons garam masala
4 tablespoons tomato purée
4 tablespoons tamarind
1 bay leaf

Put the washed tripe in a large saucepan. Cover with cold water and add the salt. Place over a medium-high heat and bring to the boil. Reduce the heat to low and simmer for 45 minutes. Drain well, reserving 4 tablespoons of the cooking liquid. Slice the tripe into wide strips and set aside.

Put the oil, onion, garlic and ginger in a saucepan large enough to eventually take the tripe. Place over a medium heat and fry until lightly golden, stirring occasionally. Reduce the heat to low. Add the spices, tomato purée, tamarind and bay leaf and simmer for 7 minutes.

Stir in the reserved cooking water and add the sliced tripe. Simmer for 15 minutes, stirring occasionally. Add salt to taste. Serve very hot with plain rice.

SERVES 4-6

TAGINE OF TRIPE

FWAD

You could vary this recipe by using sheep's heads instead of the tripe and lungs. Or if you are squeamish, you could use lamb shanks. Though if you are reading this book, you can't really be that squeamish, so I suggest you try the sheep's heads for an unusual and unexpected tagine. You will need two heads, which you will need to wash well, then singe and then wash well again before using.

1 pair lamb's lungs
1kg lamb's tripe, well washed and rinsed
2 teaspoons paprika
1½ teaspoons ground cumin
4-6 garlic cloves, crushed
Few sprigs fresh coriander, most of the stalk discarded, finely chopped
1 medium onion, finely chopped
4 tablespoons extra virgin olive oil
100g chickpeas, soaked overnight with a little bicarbonate of soda

Put the lungs under the cold water tap and run the water through the trachea to swell it and wash out the congealed blood. Dice into cubes about 3-4cm square.

Cut the tripe in pieces more or less the same size as the lungs. Blanch both tripe and lungs. Drain and put in a clean saucepan.

Add the remaining ingredients – reserve a little coriander for garnish. Add about 1½ litres water and place over a medium-high heat. Bring to the boil, then reduce the heat to medium. Boil gently for about 1½ hours, or until the tripe, lungs and chickpeas are tender and the sauce thickened. Check halfway through cooking to make sure that the sauce is not drying out. If it is, add a little water. When the tagine is done, transfer to a serving dish, sprinkle with a little chopped coriander and serve immediately with good bread.

SERVES 6

COD'S TRIPE

WITH CANNELLINI BEANS

TRIPA DI BACALLÀ

Cod's tripe is a prized and rare delicacy in the Spanish city of Barcelona. It has an interesting, rather gelatinous texture and unlike ox or lamb's tripe, it cooks in no time at all. It is sold already cured, salted and dried and if you come across it you will need to soak it for three days before using. The recipe below was given to me by señora Goma, owner of two baccallao stalls at the Boqueria market in Barcelona. She uses the classic Catalan sofregit mix as a basis for the sauce. The following recipe is very simple to prepare once you have soaked the tripe and beans. In Barcelona, and elsewhere in Spain, you can buy pulses already soaked and cooked, which is a great bonus.

250g salted and dried cod's tripe (about 4-5 pieces)
250g cannellini beans, soaked overnight with
  $1/2$ teaspoon bicarbonate of soda
4 tablespoons extra virgin olive oil
2 medium onions, finely chopped
3 garlic cloves, crushed
50g flat-leaf parsley, most of the bottom stalk
  discarded, then finely chopped
1 x 400g tin of Italian plum tomatoes, chopped
Scant 1 teaspoon finely ground white pepper
Sea salt

Three days ahead of time

Put the tripe to soak in plenty of cold water for 24 hours. Drain the tripe and transfer to a saucepan. Cover with water and place over a medium-high heat. Bring to the boil, then drain and put again to soak in cold water for 2 days. Keep in the refrigerator.

On the day

Put the olive oil in a saucepan and place over a medium heat. When the oil is hot, add the chopped onion and fry until golden-brown, stirring occasionally. This should take 15-20 minutes.

Drain and rinse the beans and put in another saucepan. Cover them well with water and bring to the boil over a medium-high heat. Then, lower the heat and simmer for 40-45 minutes, or until the beans are tender but not mushy.

When the onions are done, add the garlic and parsley and cook, stirring occasionally, for a couple of minutes. Add the tomatoes and their juice, the pepper and salt to taste and simmer for 5-10 minutes, or until you have a thick, concentrated sofregit.

Drain the cod's tripe and remove the blackish skin on the inside. This is quite fiddly but I suggest you do it as the texture of the skin is not so pleasant. Also, the presentation will be more appealing if the tripe is completely white. Cut the tripe across into medium-thin strips.

Add the tripe and drained beans to the sofregit and simmer over a very low heat for 15 minutes. If the sauce is sticking, add a little water, not too much though as you don't want the sauce to become soupy. Taste and adjust the seasoning if necessary. Serve very hot with good bread.

SERVES 4-6

STUFFED LAMB'S
TRIPE

GHAMMEH

In Lebanon you can buy both tripe and intestines already cleaned. But this is not to say that you won't need to wash them again in several changes of lightly soapy water, and then rinse them very well every time, so as to get rid of the slightly off taste. I remember how, when I lived in Lebanon, I always had to beg my mother to cook this dish. We all loved it but the preparation time was so long that my mother would always wait for a special occasion before she would agree to make it. You have been warned.

For the stuffing

200g chickpeas, soaked overnight in plenty of cold water with 1 teaspoon bicarbonate of soda
1 teaspoon bicarbonate of soda
450g short-grain rice
2 x 800g tins Italian tomatoes, drained, and coarsely chopped
500g onions (about 2 large ones), finely chopped
500g minced lamb from the neck
2 teaspoons seven-pepper mixture (or ground allspice)
$\frac{1}{2}$ teaspoon finely ground black pepper
$\frac{1}{2}$ teaspoon ground cinnamon
Sea salt

To finish

6 lamb's trotters, singed and washed
2-3 cinnamon sticks
1 medium-sized sheep's stomach, washed, rinsed and cut into pieces half the size of an A4 sheet of paper – you should have 6-7 pieces
1 full intestine, stripped of part of its fat, washed the same way as the tripe and left whole

Drain and rinse the chickpeas then rub them with the teaspoon of bicarbonate of soda. Leave for 15-20 minutes, then rinse well. The purpose of this operation is to soften the chickpeas further and shorten their cooking time.

Rinse the rice, drain and put in a large mixing bowl. Add the remaining ingredients for the stuffing and mix well.

Put the trotters in a large pot. Cover well with water and place over a medium-high heat. As the water is about to boil, skim it clean then add the cinnamon sticks, cover and cook for 30 minutes.

Sew one and a half sides of the pieces of tripe to create pockets. Fill these with the stuffing, making sure they are only three quarters full. The rice will expand during cooking. Sew up the open ends and set aside.

Now start filling the intestine. This job is quite fiddly, especially when you get to the thin end. Take one end of the intestine and invert a short length. Push a little stuffing into it with your finger. As you are doing this, more of the intestine will pull up for you to fill. Again, you want to fill the intestine loosely as the rice will expand. Tie each end of the intestine securely with a thread and rinse again.

Add the stuffed tripe and intestines to the trotters. Add more water to cover, if necessary, and salt to taste and cook for 2 hours or until tender. Serve very hot with some of the broth on the side. You can, if you want, season the accompanying broth with a little crushed garlic and lemon juice.

SERVES 6-8

FLORENTINE TRIPE STEW

TRIPPA ALLA FIORENTINA

One of the most typical Florentine dishes, trippa alla Fiorentina used to be sold on the street off carts wheeled by the 'trippa', specialist tripe sellers.

600g ox tripe, washed very well in soapy water, rinsed and left to soak in salted boiling water
1 calf's foot, singed and washed
Sea salt
100ml extra virgin olive oil
100g unsalted butter
2 small onions, finely chopped
1 garlic clove, finely chopped
2 tablespoons tomato purée
1 beef stock cube
3 tablespoons grated Parmesan
$\frac{1}{4}$ teaspoon grated nutmeg
Freshly ground black pepper to taste
4 pieces of toasted bread

Boil the tripe in salted water for 1 hour. Add the calf's foot and cook for another hour.

Remove the tripe and calf's foot from the pan. Bone the foot and cut into bite-sized pieces. Slice the tripe into medium long, medium-thin strips.

Put the oil and half the butter in a saucepan and place over a medium-low heat. Add half the chopped onion and half the garlic and cook until lightly golden.

Add the tomato purée, beef stock cube and 450ml of water. Simmer for 45 minutes.

Put the remaining butter, onion and garlic in a large saucepan and place over medium-low heat. Cook until lightly golden, then add the tripe and calf's foot and cook, stirring occasionally, for 10 minutes. Add some of the tomato sauce, the nutmeg and salt and pepper to taste. Simmer, stirring regularly, for 45 minutes, adding more sauce as you go along until you have used it all up. If the sauce is not enough, add a little tripe cooking broth. Stir in the grated cheese.

Place the toasted bread onto a serving platter. Spoon the tripe over the toast and serve immediately.

SERVES 4

THE SUCCULENT
TRIPE
OF CA L'ISIDRE

LOS SUCCULENTOS CALLOS DE CA L'ISIDRE

Ca l'Isidre started life more than 30 years ago as a simple tapas bar in one of Barcelona's poorest quarters, Barri Xino (now renamed Raval but still pretty seedy). Over the years, Isidre and his wife expanded their bar into an elegant restaurant that now counts King Juan Carlos as one of its faithful patrons. I was lucky enough to be taken there by a friend who has been a regular from the days when the restaurant was still a small tapas bar. He arranged for us to have an offal degustation: kid's kidneys, brains, sweetbreads, escalope de foie de canard and of course callos. Isidre's is the best tripe I have ever had in Spain and here is their recipe.

6 tablespoons extra virgin olive oil
1 large onion, finely chopped
1 head garlic, cloves separated and peeled
1 ham bone
1 bouquet garni (thyme and laurel)
150g jabugo ham, sliced into thin strips or diced into small cubes depending on how you buy it
150g thin chorizo, sliced medium-thick
2 ripe tomatoes, peeled, seeded and finely chopped
1-2 dried chilli peppers (guindilla), crushed fine
2 teaspoons Spanish paprika (pimenton dulce)
1kg cooked tripe, half honeycomb and half regular, cut into pieces about 4cm square
2-3 tablespoons flour
100ml white wine

Put the olive oil in a large saucepan and place over a medium heat. When the oil is hot, add the chopped onion and the garlic and cook, stirring occasionally, until golden.

Add the ham bone, bouquet garni, ham and chorizo and sauté for a minute or so. Add the tomatoes, chilli pepper and paprika and simmer for 5 minutes.
Add the tripe and sprinkle the flour all over. Stir well. Then add the white wine. Let it bubble for a minute or two then add 750ml water. Reduce the heat and simmer for 2-3 hours, depending on how low you can get your fire. Stir occasionally, especially towards the end of cooking. The sauce should not reduce so much as thicken. If you feel that the tripe is starting to stick, take it off the heat.

Serve very hot with good bread. When the dish cools, the sauce will set in a jelly. Re-heat it over a very low heat, adding a little water as you do so.

SERVES 4-6

TRIPE
IN THE STYLE OF
CAEN

TRIPE À LA MODE DE CAEN

The traditional way of making tripe à la mode de Caen is in a tripière, a wide earthenware pot with a cover. The lid is hermetically sealed with a paste made with flour and water, and the tripière is then placed overnight in a very slow oven. The broth should never come to the boil, but simply simmer. You can also achieve this slow-cooking on the top of the stove, using a heavy-bottomed saucepan. The very best tripe à la mode de Caen that I have ever had was at the restaurant Pharamond in Paris before it changed hands. They served the tripe in extravagantly deep plates, each over its own individual brazier which kept it hot. It was sublime.

1 piece of pork skin
1 medium onion, quartered
1 small leek, trimmed and washed
4 garlic cloves
1 clove
1 teaspoon freshly ground black pepper
1 sprig thyme
1 bay leaf
1 sprig flat-leaf parsley
1kg ox tripe, including all four types (see page137)
    blanched and cut into pieces about 5cm square
1 calf's foot, blanched and cut in two
    (ask your butcher to do this for you)
250g carrots, sliced into thin roundels
250ml medium-dry cider
Sea salt
1 tablespoon Calvados

Line the bottom of your saucepan or tripière with the pork skin.

Put a layer of tripe over the pork skin and cover with a layer of carrots and half the calf's foot. Wrap the onion, leek, peeled garlic, clove, pepper and herbs in cheesecloth and place in the pot. Cover with another layer of tripe, carrots and the other half of the foot.

Add the cider and enough water to cover the tripe well and place over a low heat. Add salt to taste and simmer, covered, for at least $2\frac{1}{2}$ hours before uncovering to check the liquid. The tripe needs to be completely immersed or else it will blacken. Cook until the tripe and foot are very tender. When the tripe is ready, remove the package containing the aromates. Remove the bones from the foot and return the meat to the pan. Stir in the Calvados. Serve very hot in soup plates with a good baguette.

SERVES 4

FEET AND PARCELS

PIEDS ET PAQUETS

Here is a wonderful classic French recipe, a speciality of Provence and in particular Marseille. The French tripe butchers (tripiers) have a way of making the paquets which is quite different from the way I explain below. They manage to fold the tripe in such a way so that the filling is securely encased without the need to sew the tripe. But I haven't been able to replicate the method at home, so I suggest that you make the paquets by simply sewing them. This recipe comes from a little-known book written by two anonymous writers who signed themselves as Bifrons. It is a time-consuming recipe and, depending on how clean the uncooked tripe is when you buy it, can take up to one hour cleaning before you can even start to cook. In short, allow half a day's work. Perhaps you can rope in a helper, as I do when my mother is visiting. Still, it is well worth the trouble as the finished dish is perfectly delightful.

1 lamb's stomach, scrubbed very clean and then washed in soapy water and rinsed thoroughly
6 lamb's feet or 1½ calf's feet
120ml extra virgin olive oil
4-5 garlic cloves, crushed
2 bunches Swiss chard (about 800g), leaves only
400g baby spinach
200g flat-leaf parsley, leaves only
200g chervil, leaves only
100g short-grain rice, rinsed and drained
150g walnuts, coarsely chopped
6 organic eggs
200g grated Parmesan
1½ teaspoons finely ground white pepper
1 teaspoon quatre-épices (optional)
Sea salt
2 medium onions, thinly sliced
450g garden carrots, quartered lengthways then cut across in half
1 x 800g tin Italian plum tomatoes, coarsely chopped
2 bay leaves
300ml dry white wine
50g basil, leaves only

Heat half the olive oil in a large saucepan over a medium-high heat. Add the garlic and greens and cook for 10-15 minutes, stirring regularly, until the greens wilt. Remove from the heat and let cool.

While the greens are cooling, start making the paquets. Cut the lamb's stomach in pieces measuring about 14cm x 8-10cm. Sew on two sides leaving the third one open so that you can fill them. It won't be possible to cut all the pieces to the same shape but as long as the paquets are all approximately the same size you will be alright. You should end up with about 15 small paquets. You can make them bigger, but the presentation will not be as appealing.

Strain and discard the juices from the cooled greens, then add the rice. Add the walnuts, eggs and Parmesan and mix well. Add ½ teaspoon of the pepper, the four-spice mixture, if you are using it, and salt to taste. Fill the paquets with the mixture, but only three quarters full as the rice will expand. Sew the opening.

Heat the rest of the olive oil in a large casserole over a medium heat. Add the sliced onion and sauté until golden. Add the carrots and tomatoes and cook for 5 minutes. Lay as many of the filled paquets as will fit comfortably over the vegetables. Lay the feet over them and cover with the rest of the paquets. Add the wine and let bubble for a couple of minutes before covering the meat with warm water. Make sure the tripe parcels are completely covered with water or else they will blacken. Put the lid on and cook for 2½ hours or until the tripe and feet are done.

When the tripe and feet are cooked, remove the feet onto a plate. Bone them and cut the meat in medium-sized pieces. Transfer the tripe parcels to a bowl and keep covered. Strain the sauce. Wipe the pan clean then return the strained sauce, tripe parcels and boned feet to the pan. Add the remaining pepper and salt to taste and bring back to the boil. Cook for another 5-10 minutes. Turn off the heat and stir in the basil leaves. Serve immediately or let the sauce set in a jelly to serve at room temperature.

SERVES 6-8

PIG'S STOMACH
WITH SAMFAINA AND CANNELLINI BEANS

*VENTRES DE PORC AMB
SAMFAINA I MONGETA SECA*

In France, pig's stomach is used solely in the making of andouilles and andouillettes, whereas in Spain it is sold ready-cooked to be used more or less like ox tripe. I rather like the texture of pig's stomach. It is firmer and has more crunch than either lamb's or ox. I am indebted to Señora Maria Font i Llupia for providing me with this wonderful recipe.

500g cannellini beans, soaked overnight with
  1 teaspoon of bicarbonate of soda
Samfaina ('Ratatouille' 1, see page 123)
2 cooked pig's stomachs (about 500g), cut into strips

Rinse and drain the beans and put in a saucepan. Cover well with water and place over a medium heat. Bring to the boil, then lower the heat and simmer for 45 minutes.

Prepare the samfaina as explained on page 123, using a saucepan large enough to eventually take the pig's stomachs and the beans.

Drain the beans and add to the samfaina. Add the pig's stomachs. Mix carefully and simmer for 20 minutes, adding a little water if the sauce is getting too dry. Serve very hot.

SERVES 4-6

RIGATONI WITH INTESTINES ROMAN STYLE

RIGATONI CON LA PAJATA

Pajata is a small part of the intestines of veal or lamb, which contains, as it is known in Italian, the chimo, a tasty substance which is left untouched when the intestines are cleaned. It is part of the very upper section of the intestine, where the bits of grass that the calf has grazed on have only been partially digested. These small bits of chewed grass, called paja in dialect, are what give this dish its name.

4 tablespoons extra virgin olive oil
1 medium onion, finely chopped
1 celery stalk, finely chopped
90g ham fat, diced very small
2 cloves garlic
A handful flat-leaf parsley, finely chopped
1.5kg pajata, cut into 25cm segments and the ends
    tied together with thread so that they look like
    bracelets
Sea salt and freshly ground black pepper
250ml dry white wine
3 tablespoons tomato purée
400g rigatoni
90g mature Pecorino, grated

Put the oil in a large saucepan and place over a low heat. When the oil is hot, add the onion, celery, ham fat, garlic and parsley and fry until the onion is golden.

Remove the garlic cloves and add the pajata. Season with salt and pepper to taste and cook until the meat is browned.

Add the wine and reduce until almost completely evaporated. Add the tomato purée and enough water to cover. Simmer, covered, for about 1 hour. Check the water halfway during cooking. If the sauce is getting too dry, add a little hot water. You want the sauce to be quite thick.

Put some salted water to boil and 10 minutes before the pajata is ready, cook the rigatoni until al dente.

Drain the rigatoni. Transfer to a serving bowl and mix with half the pajata. Arrange the remaining pajata over the pasta and serve immediately with the grated Pecorino.

SERVES 4-6

PIG'S SNOUT, EARS AND TAIL STEW WITH PEAS

MORRO, ORELLA I CUA DE PORC AMB PESOLS

Some English butchers are not very good at selling you clean pig's heads. I nearly gave up on testing this recipe, which I was given by Senora Maria Font i Llupia, when I unpacked the pig's head I had ordered from my local butcher. The skin was hairy, the snout full of snot and the ears caked with wax. Revolting! But I wasn't about to give up on it, so I put the head in the sink and started scraping and washing it until I had it as clean as you would find it in an Italian, French, Spanish or conscientious English butcher.

There is a wonderful scene in the film *La Grande Bouffe*, where the actor Michel Piccoli starts dancing with a calf's head held against his cheeks, while Ugo Tognazzi is taking delivery of the rest of the meat for their weekend blow out. I could have done the same with mine, had the pig's head my butcher gave me been as clean as the head Michel Piccoli was cradling. Still, hard work was rewarded as the resulting stew was quite wonderful. So the lesson of this story is that before attempting this recipe, and for the sake of ease and sanity, you must insist that your butcher clean the head really well before letting you have it. And then, perhaps, the dancing can begin.

6 tablespoons extra virgin olive oil
1 medium onion, very finely chopped
2 cloves garlic, very finely chopped
2 medium ripe tomatoes, peeled, seeded and chopped
1 pig's ear, cut into bite-sized pieces
1 pig's snout, cut into bite-sized pieces
1 pig's tail, cut into small chunks
Sea salt and freshly ground black pepper
500g fresh peas or equivalent frozen
$1/4$ teaspoon nutmeg

Put the oil in a large saucepan and place over a medium heat. When the oil is hot, add the onion and sauté until golden. Add the garlic and when it is slightly coloured, add the tomatoes and cook until all liquid evaporates and the sauce is very thick.

Add the meats and cover with water. Season with salt and pepper to taste. Simmer for 1 to $1^{1}/_{2}$ hours, or until the meat is tender and the broth reduced. Add the peas and nutmeg and cook for a further 10 minutes, or until the peas are done. Serve immediately.

SERVES 4-6

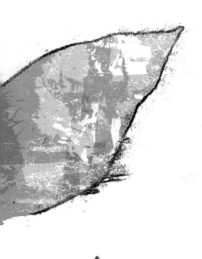

RED-COOKED BRAINS

HONGSHAO NAOHUA

Pig's brains are normally reserved for special occasions in the Szechwan province of China, and are a delicacy certainly worth trying to source for this spicy dish. The Chinese cookery writer, Mrs Chiang, whose recipe this is, suggests using calf's brains if all efforts to find pig's fail.

700g pig's brains (or 2 whole calf's brains)
4 spring onions, trimmed and thinly sliced
4cm piece of fresh ginger, peeled and finely chopped
Fine sea salt
1¼ teaspoons caster sugar
2 teaspoons sesame oil
3 tablespoons soy sauce
2 teaspoons roasted Szechwan peppers, ground
2 tablespoons Chinese rice wine
5 tablespoons peanut oil
8 cloves garlic, finely chopped
2 tablespoons hot pepper paste
1½ tablespoons cornflour

Rinse the brains under cold water. Pat dry and slice across in 2½cm thick pieces. Place in a large bowl.

Add the onion, ginger, salt to taste, sugar, sesame oil, peppers and rice wine, and carefully mix the brains in with the seasonings. Cover and let marinate for 20 minutes.

Put the wok over a high heat and let it heat for about 15 seconds. Add the peanut oil and when the oil starts smoking, add the garlic. Stir-fry for 30 seconds, making sure it doesn't burn.

Quickly stir in the hot pepper paste, then add the brains and their marinade and stir-fry for 1 minute. Dilute the cornflour in 1 tablespoon of water and add to the pan. Cover the pan and cook, stirring occasionally for 3 minutes. Serve immediately with plain rice.

SERVES 4

SHEEP'S HEAD ROLL

I found this recipe in Marguerite Patten's *Victory Cookbook*, re-issued by Hamlyn in 1995. One of the main reasons why offal went out of fashion in Britain after the second world war was that it had become the only meat readily available during the years of rationing. The association of offal with hard times probably explains why the British turned away from it once meat became more widely available again.

1 sheep's head, split in half by your butcher but
  with the two halves still attached
1 tablespoon vinegar
2 cloves
1 blade of mace
1 cinnamon stick
1 garlic clove
1 tablespoon chopped mixed herbs
450g turnips, peeled and diced
450g carrots, peeled and diced
Sea salt and freshly ground black pepper
100g brown breadcrumbs
100g flour

Soak the sheep's head in water for about an hour. Drain and rinse well, then tie in cheesecloth to stop the cut head from opening during cooking. Put in a large pot and cover with cold water. Place over a medium heat and bring to the boil. Discard the water and wipe the pan clean. Rinse the sheep's head and return to the pan. Add the seasonings and vegetables. Cover with water and simmer for 2 hours, or until the meat falls off the bone.

Strain the head and vegetables, reserving the stock for later use. Untie the head and take the meat off the bone. Peel and slice the tongue and set aside. Mince the rest of the meat and blend with the vegetables, breadcrumbs and flour. Taste and adjust the seasoning if necessary

Flour your hands and press the meat into a long, wide strip. Arrange the tongue slices down the middle and shape into a roll. Wrap the roll in cheesecloth and steam for an hour. Let cool before unwrapping. Slice and serve with a mixed leaf salad.

SERVES 4

CRAPPIT HEADS

Here is Catherine Brown's modern take on crappit heads, published in her book *Scottish Regional Recipes*. In it she explains that when very large cod, haddock or other similar white fish are caught, every scrap is used. Hence this method of making an oatmeal pudding with the flavourful fish liver stuffed into the head. The liver melts into the oatmeal as it cooks and the head adds its own flavour to this unique Highland dish. The old Scots word 'crap' means to 'fill' or 'stuff'.

4 large fish heads
Fish liver
Oatmeal
Onion or spring onion, finely chopped
Sea salt and freshly ground black pepper

Place the fish liver in a bowl and cover with cold water. Add some salt and soak for an hour. Strain. Add enough oatmeal and onion to the fish liver to make a fairly thick consistency. Season to taste.

Place the mixture in a cleaned head and tie up with string. Begin by tying a sort of noose round the mouth to keep the jaws shut then take the string over the head and make another noose round the centre of the head. Finally tie up the remains of the stomach bag at the back of the head. Wrap in foil and put in a pan of boiling water. Simmer for 30 minutes. Serve the head on its own or with a portion of plain boiled cod. If the head is not available, the mixture can be boiled in a cloth.

SERVES 4

FISH HEAD CURRY

GULAI KEPALA IKAN

This extraordinary curry is regarded by most as one of Singapore's national dishes, although not all will agree. If you listen to some, they will say that it was Gomez, an Indian cook living in Singapore who invented the dish in the 1950s having decided that it was too much of a waste to throw away fish heads, choosing instead to cook them. But if you listen to others, you will be told that the dish could not have been invented by an Indian as Indians do not normally cook fish heads as meals in themelves. Whatever the truth, this was a great favourite of one of my dearest friends, Donald Munson, who lived in Singapore for a while, where I would visit him and where he would cook this dish. Sadly, he died before he could give me his recipe for Fish Head Curry, so I resorted to searching for a recipe that would do justice to the one he cooked for me, eventually finding it on an excellent food website called Asia On-line.

850g fish heads, cut into 2-4 pieces
Lime juice
Sea salt
2 tablespoons desiccated coconut, roasted
   and pounded
1 tablespoon coriander seeds
$\frac{1}{2}$ teaspoon cumin seeds
$\frac{1}{4}$ teaspoon anise seeds
1 teaspoon peppercorns
10 dried red chillies, or to taste
$\frac{1}{2}$ tablespoon chopped turmeric
$\frac{1}{2}$ tablespoon chopped ginger
7 shallots
3 garlic cloves
1 tablespoon dried star fruit (or tamarind juice)
3 tablespoons vegetable oil
1 stalk lemon grass, bruised
1 pandanus leaf, torn and knotted
750ml coconut milk from 1 coconut
5 star fruit, halved
10 salam leaves (Indonesian bay leaves but you
   can use regular ones)

Rub the fish head pieces with lime juice and salt. Let sit for 30 minutes. Drain the fish head and rub with the pounded coconut.

Put the coriander, cumin, anise seeds and peppercorns in a dry pan and sauté until the aroma rises. Be careful not to let the spices burn. Let them cool, then grind together with the dried chillies, shallots, garlic and star fruit until fine.

Heat the oil in a saucepan large enough to eventually take the fish heads and sauté the ground spices, lemon grass and pandanus leaf until the aroma rises. Add the coconut milk and let simmer for a few minute

Add the fish head and star fruit, and bring to the boil, stirring occasionally. Add the salam leaves and simmer until the fish is cooked and the gravy is a little oily, about half an hour. Serve hot with plain rice.

SERVES 2-4

A HEAD DINNER FOR TWO

STARTER
POACHED BRAIN AND EYES WITH FLEUR DE SEL

MIDDLE COURSE
LAMB'S TONGUE
WITH VINAIGRETTE SAUCE

MAIN COURSE
LAMB'S CHEEKS WITH BLANQUETTE SAUCE

The above menu may sound outrageous but I can assure you that it is not only delicious but also remarkably refined.

When I tested and served this head feast in Paris, during a hot summer spell when temperatures were in the high 90s, my dutiful guest was, to say the least, quite surprised. He made the de rigueur disparaging remarks about offal, 'What, offal in this heat? Are you mad? When will you finish this book?' (I had to put up with many such remarks throughout most of the writing of *The Fifth Quarter*.) But, by the end of the meal and to my huge satisfaction, he had changed his opinion.

Should you decide to take the plunge and try preparing this meal, you will need to ask your butcher for a sheep's head and two extra tongues with the cheeks still attached to them. Ideally, the head should be split only partially so that the brain remains protected during cooking. The split will also allow you to open the head with ease after it is cooked.

Place the head and tongues to soak overnight, changing the water as often as you can. The next day, separate the cheeks from the tongues, trim them if necessary and set aside.

Put the head and tongues in a large pot, add one large onion studded with 3 cloves, one leek, one large branch of celery, preferably with the leaves attached, a handful of flat-leaf parsley, 3 sprigs of thyme and one large bay leaf. Cover the meats with 4 litres of water and add 4 tablespoons of sea salt. Bring to the boil, skim the surface clean, and then lower the heat and simmer for 1½ hours.

Put the cheeks in another small saucepan together with a small onion studded with 2 cloves, a small carrot which you have quartered, a branch of celery and a bouquet garni made with fresh thyme, parsley and a bay leaf. Add 500ml water and place over a medium-low heat. As the water is about to come to the boil, skim the surface clean. Make sure you remove all the scum, as you will be using the stock later to make the blanquette sauce – you want the stock to be really clear. Add 1 tablespoon of salt and four peppercorns. Simmer for 1 hour.

While the meats are cooking, prepare the vinaigrette on page 128. Pick the leaves off a few sprigs of tarragon and set them aside until you are ready to serve the vinaigrette.

A few minutes before the cheeks are ready, start making the blanquette sauce on page 127 and when it is ready, add the meat and onions. Keep warm.

Take the tongues out of the pan. Cut off and discard the glands and the extra meat at the bottom and sides. Peel the skin off while still hot, and then wrap in a clean kitchen cloth and set aside. Arrange a few washed and dried lettuce leaves on two separate plates and place in the refrigerator.

Take the head out of the stock and remove the cheeks. Add these to the blanquette sauce. Gently prize the skull open and remove the brains. Divide the brains between two plates. Take the eyes out of the head. Now carefully remove and discard the black bit in the middle of each eye and place an eye on each plate next to the brains. Serve immediately with fleur de sel, or other very good salt.

After you have eaten the brains and eyes, it is time to serve the tongues. Slice these open lengthways, leaving them attached at the bottom. Open them out and lay two each, cut side up, on the lettuce leaves. Mix the tarragon into the vinaigrette, drizzle all over and serve.

Finish with the cheeks in the blanquette sauce and serve with good bread. And there you have it, an all-offal meal that will certainly surprise your guest but will also delight him or her with its delicate textures and tastes.

4

BARBECUES

PIG'S LIVER KEBABS

FEGATELLI DI MAIALE ALLA BOLOGNESE

Pig's liver is much more prized in Italy than it is in the rest of Europe. I have yet to decide whether I like it or not. The taste is strong although not so strong as to make it unpalatable. Still, if I have the choice, I would always go for lamb's or calf's liver, but here is an excellent recipe for those who would like to try it.

150ml extra virgin olive oil
Juice of 1/2 lemon, or to taste
1 tablespoon dried rosemary
1 tablespoon dried sage
1 pig's liver, diced into 2 1/2 cm cubes
Sea salt and freshly ground black pepper
Fresh sage leaves
1 piece of fresh caul large enough to cut in big
   enough squares to wrap each of the 6 brochettes
6 slices good country bread, toasted

Put wooden skewers to soak in water.

Mix the oil, lemon juice, rosemary and sage in a large mixing bowl. Add the cubes of liver. Season with salt and pepper to taste and let marinate in a cool place for 2 hours, stirring occasionally.

Thread the pieces of liver in equal quantities onto 6 skewers, inserting a sage leaf in between each cube of meat.

Wrap the brochettes with the caul and place under a pre-heated grill or over a barbecue. Cook for 2-3 minutes on each side, or until the liver is done to your liking. Baste with the marinade during cooking to keep the liver moist.

Place each brochette on a piece of toasted bread. Serve immediately with a mixed salad.

SERVES 4-6

HEART KEBABS

BROCHETTES DE COEUR

This is an excellent way to serve heart, though you must be careful not to grill the meat for too long as it will become tough.

750g ox or calf's heart, trimmed and diced into
   1½cm cubes
1 tablespoon extra virgin olive oil
Juice of 1 lemon, or to taste
4 sprigs flat-leaf parsley, finely chopped
Sea salt and freshly ground pepper, to taste
Herb butter on page 128

Put 12 wooden skewers to soak in water.

Mix the heart pieces with the seasonings in a large mixing bowl. Let marinate for 1 hour, stirring occasionally.

Prepare the butter while the meat is marinating. Thread the pieces of meat onto the wooden skewers and grill under a pre-heated grill or over a barbecue for 8 minutes, turning the brochettes so that the meat browns all over. Serve immediately with good bread and the herb butter.

SERVES 4

MOROCCAN LIVER & HEART KEBABS

QOTBANE DEL'KEBDA WA L'QALB

Moroccans traditionally use the fat from the tail of fat-tail sheep on these kebabs, but, sadly, you will not find any fat-tail sheep here in England. So, I suggest you use fat taken from around the kidneys, or even none at all. In the absence of the moistening effect of fat, simply brush the meat with a little olive oil or melted butter during grilling. On the streets of Morocco you can buy these spicy brochettes slipped off their skewers and stuffed into Moroccan bread, which makes for a very tasty sandwich.

500g lamb's liver, trimmed and diced into
   smallish cubes
500g lamb's hearts, trimmed and diced into
   smallish cubes
200g fat from the tail of sheep, diced into
   smallish cubes (optional)
2 garlic cloves, crushed
1 tablespoon finely chopped parsley
1 teaspoon ground cumin
1½ teaspoons paprika
Sea salt

Put 12 wooden skewers to soak in water.

Put the meat and fat (if using) in a large mixing bowl. Add the garlic, parsley and seasonings and let marinate for at least 1 hour, stirring the meats regularly.

Thread the meat onto the skewers, alternating the different meats. Grill over a charcoal fire or under a pre-heated grill for 3-4 minutes on each side, or less if the heat is strong. You do not want to overcook the meat as it will toughen. Serve immediately with a large salad and Moroccan bread if you can find it.

SERVES 6

LAMB'S LIVER KEBABS WRAPPED IN CAUL

BOULFAF

Here is a very nice variation on simple liver kebabs. The liver is first seared and then cut up, and the pieces then wrapped in caul before being skewered and grilled. The liver pieces thus stay moist inside the caul, which then adds another texture to the kebabs.

Extra virgin olive oil
1 lamb's liver
1 large piece of caul, cut in strips, each wide enough to wrap the cubes of liver
1½ teaspoons paprika
1 teaspoon ground cumin
few sprigs flat-leaf parsley, most of the stalks discarded, then finely chopped
1 garlic clove, crushed
Sea salt to taste

Put 12 wooden skewers to soak.

Put a little olive oil in a frying pan and place over a medium-high heat. When the oil is hot, add the liver and sear on both sides for 2-3 minutes each. Cut the liver in two lengthwise and sear the cut sides.

Remove the liver onto a chopping board and dice into cubes about 4cm square. Transfer to a large mixing bowl. Add the caul and seasonings and mix well. Marinate for 1 hour at least, stirring regularly.

Wrap a strip of caul around a liver cube and thread on a skewer. Carry on wrapping and threading the cubes of liver until you use up all the liver and caul.

Grill over a charcoal fire or under a pre-heated grill for 3-4 minutes on each side, or until done to your liking, bearing in mind that you do not want to overcook the liver as it will go hard and rubbery. Serve immediately with a mixed salad, good bread and the harissa on page 122 if you like your kebabs spicy.

SERVES 4-6

INTESTINE BROCHETTES
SARDINIAN STYLE

CORDULA

This is an ancient and unusual dish that has been part of the fare of Sardinian shepherds for centuries. It bears a certain resemblance to the South American chinchulines – the uncleaned intestines of milk-fed calves, which are rolled together into a large disc and then barbecued over charcoal. I once tried chinchulines in Argentina where they form part of an asado (mixed grill) and they were utterly delicious. I was amazed at how remarkably free the intestines were of any alien odour or taste, considering that they had not been emptied. The idea of simply grilling intestines does not exist in France or in Lebanon, although I have seen grilled intestines in the markets in Morocco, where they are called kerdes. Moroccans also prepare intestines for the barbecue by cutting them in 1cm sections, seasoning them and then threading them onto skewers before grilling.

The intestines of 2 lambs
Few sprigs of fresh marjoram, leaves only, very finely chopped
Few sprigs thyme, leaves only
2-3 sprigs sage, leaves only, very finely chopped
1 bay leaf, crumbled
Sea salt and freshly ground pepper
150g pork back fat

Undo the intestines, both large and small, and clean them by turning them inside out and washing them in several changes of soapy water. Rinse well. Season with the herbs and salt and pepper to taste. Tress them and thread the tresses onto 6 long skewers.

Melt the pork fat and dribble it all over the meat. Grill under a pre-heated grill or over a barbecue fire for 15-20 minutes, turning the brochettes so that the meat browns all over. Serve immediately with good bread and a mixed salad.

SERVES 6

ITALIAN OFFAL TRESSES

TORCINELLI

This recipe is similar to the Greek/Turkish Kokoretsi/Kokoreç (recipe following), except that the Italian version is flavoured with sage while the Greeks use oregano and the Turks spices. All are delicious.

400g lamb's lights (heart, lungs and liver), diced into 2.5cm cubes
Sea salt and freshly ground black pepper
400g lamb's intestines, washed very well and rinsed
1-2 sprigs sage
Extra virgin olive oil
Juice of 1 lemon, or to taste

Put 6 wooden skewers to soak in water.

Season the pieces of light with salt and pepper to taste and thread them onto the skewers, alternating the heart, lung and liver pieces and putting a sage leaf in between every 3 pieces.

Tie one end of the intestine around the top end of the skewer and bring it down to cover one side of the meat. Tie it around the skewer just under the meat and bring it back up to cover the other side. Repeat until the meat is covered on all sides. Do the same with the remaining skewers. Brush them all with olive oil and grill under a pre-heated grill or over a barbecue fire for 15-20 minutes Turn the skewers often, brushing the meat with oil at regular intervals. Slide off the skewers onto a serving platter. Sprinkle with a little lemon juice and serve immediately with a salad or a vegetable of your choice and good bread.

SERVES 6

GREEK KOKORETSI

This is the Greek variation on Torcinelli, a kind of fresh andouillette but filled with kidney and sheep's pluck. This recipe was given to me by Rena Salaman, author of *Greek Food*. Kokoretsi is traditionally grilled over a charcoal fire, but you can also cook it under a regular grill or over a gas fire. The Turks have a similar version which they call Kokoreç.

1 sheep's pluck and kidney (or 2, if small)
Dried oregano
Sea salt and freshly ground black pepper
Lamb's intestines, washed very well and rinsed
Extra virgin olive oil
Juice of 1 lemon

Rinse and drain the sheep's pluck before dicing the meat into cubes about 5cm square. Season with oregano, salt and pepper to taste and thread onto one long skewer, alternating the pieces, until you have used them all.

Tie one end of the intestine around the top end of the skewer and bring it down to cover one side of the meat. Tie it around the skewer just under the meat and bring it back up to cover the other side. Repeat until the meat is covered on all sides. After which start wrapping the intestine round the meat in a spiral. The more intestine you have around the meat, the better.

Mix a little olive oil with the lemon juice and brush the kokoretsi with it. Season with more salt, pepper and oregano and grill slowly, brushing occasionally with the olive oil and lemon mixture until the meat is cooked through. Serve immediately with a mixed salad.

SERVES 2-4

5

SAUCES &
DIPS

HOT CHILLI DIP

HARISSA

Most people think of harissa as Moroccan but it is actually Tunisian and is used there as a sandwich spread in the same way that we use butter, mayonnaise or mustard. Harissa is also served as a dip, drizzled with olive oil. In homes it is generally served plain, while in restaurants it is topped with canned tuna and olives. Commercial harissa, especially that sold in tubes, does not compare to that which is home-made. It is well worth finding good chilli peppers to make your own.

240g large dried chilli peppers
15-20 garlic cloves, peeled
Fine sea salt
1/2 cup caraway seeds, ground
Extra virgin olive oil to cover the harissa

Pull off the stalks of the peppers. Shake out and discard the loose seeds. Rinse the peppers and soak in hot water for about 20 minutes.

Put the garlic in a food processor with a little salt. Process until very smooth.

Drain the peppers, add to the garlic and pulse until you have a lightly textured paste. The peppers should not be completely pulverised.

Transfer to a mixing bowl. Add the ground caraway and more salt if necessary and mix well. Store in a glass jar, covered with olive oil. The oil helps preserve the harissa and without it, it will go mouldy very quickly. Make sure you top up the oil every time you use some of the harissa. This way, it will keep for months in the refrigerator.

MAKES ABOUT 350g

GARLIC DIP

THÜM

This is the Lebanese version of aioli, but without any egg. Thüm is an extremely pungent dip which should be used in moderation, for fear of the consumers becoming social lepers for some days following.

5 large garlic cloves
Sea salt
90ml extra virgin olive oil
3-4 tablespoons strained yogurt
1 medium potato, boiled and mashed

Put the peeled garlic cloves and a little salt in a mortar and pound with a pestle until reduced to a very fine paste.

Drizzle in the oil, very slowly, stirring constantly as if you were making mayonnaise. Add the strained yogurt and mashed potatoes and mix well.

MAKES ABOUT 100ml

CATALAN 'RATATOUILLE' 1
FROM SENORA FONT LLUPIA

SAMFAINA 1 DE SEÑORA FONT LLUPIA

Samfaina is the Catalan equivalent of ratatouille. It can be eaten on its own or used as a sauce for many dishes. It is simple to prepare, but takes rather a long time to cook. Each ingredient is added separately and left to soften before the next is added. The whole mixture is then left to stew until it turns to a mush, quite unlike ratatouille. I am giving two versions here, both from wonderful cooks in Barcelona. The first is from Señora Font Llupia, the proud mother of the most handsome charcutiers in Mercat Sant Antoni, while the second is from Albert Sim, the owner-cook of the celebrated Bar Pinotxo in the Boqueria market in Barcelona.

6 tablespoons extra virgin olive oil
200g red pepper, trimmed and thinly sliced
450g aubergines, diced into 1cm cubes
200g onion, very finely chopped
200g courgettes, sliced into very thin roundels
100g green pepper, trimmed and thinly sliced
4 medium ripe tomatoes (about 300g), peeled,
   seeded and finely chopped
1 teaspoon sugar
Sea salt and pepper to taste

Put the oil in a saucepan and place over a low heat. When the oil is hot, add the red pepper and cook covered, stirring occasionally, for 15 minutes.

Add the aubergines and let soften for 15 minutes. Add the onions and courgettes. Cook for 15 minutes.

Add the green peppers. By now the vegetables should be stewing in their own juices and the skins from the peppers should have come loose. Pick these out of the sauce, then add the tomatoes. Simmer for 45 minutes. Stir every now and then and mash the vegetables until they have lost their shape.

CATALAN 'RATATOUILLE' 2
FROM ALBERT SIM

SAMFAINA 2 DE ALBERT SIM

8 tablespoons extra virgin olive oil
125g red pepper, trimmed and thinly sliced
125g green pepper, trimmed and thinly sliced
250g onion, very finely chopped
250g aubergines, diced into 1cm cubes
250g courgettes, sliced into very thin roundels
3-4 medium tomatoes (about 250g), peeled, seeded
   and finely chopped
1 teaspoon sugar
1 teaspoon Spanish paprika (pimenton dulce)
Sea salt and freshly ground black pepper, to taste

Put the oil in a saucepan and place over low heat. When the oil is hot, add the peppers and onions and cook, stirring occasionally, for 15-20 minutes.

Add the aubergines, cover the pan and leave to soften for 15 minutes, then add the courgettes. Cook for another 15 minutes. By now the vegetables should be stewing in their own juices and the skins from the peppers should have come loose. Pick these out of the sauce.

Add the tomatoes and simmer for 45 minutes. Stir occasionally and mash the vegetables until they have lost their shape. If the vegetables stick to the bottom of the pan, add a little water.

TOMATO SAUCE

CREME D'ARTICHAUT

This sauce goes with so many dishes, but particularly with the boiled ox tongue on page 58 as well as with any dish featuring sautéed lamb's or chicken livers, with or without the cornichons and capers.

5 tablespoons extra virgin olive oil
1 medium onion, very finely chopped
3 x 800g tins Italian tomatoes
1 bouquet garni (thyme and laurel)
Sea salt and freshly ground pepper
18 cornichons, extra fine, sliced lengthways into
    very thin slices.
3 tablespoons capers, rinsed

Put the oil in a saucepan and place over a medium heat. When the oil is hot, add the onion and fry, stirring occasionally, until golden.

Add the tomatoes and bouquet garni, season with salt and pepper to taste and simmer for an hour or until the sauce is reduced by half.

Pass the sauce through a fine sieve and return to the pan. Add the cornichons and capers and simmer for 5 more minutes.

This is a lovely, silky sauce that goes very well with the chicken liver mousse on page 28, but also marries very well with any number of other liver dishes.

3 large artichoke hearts, cleaned and finely chopped
100ml crème fraîche
Sea salt
100ml extra virgin olive oil
Few sprigs flat-leaf parsley, finely chopped

Put the artichoke hearts and cream in a saucepan. Add salt to taste and simmer until the artichokes are tender. Liquidise and let cool.

Whisk in the olive oil and then the parsley.

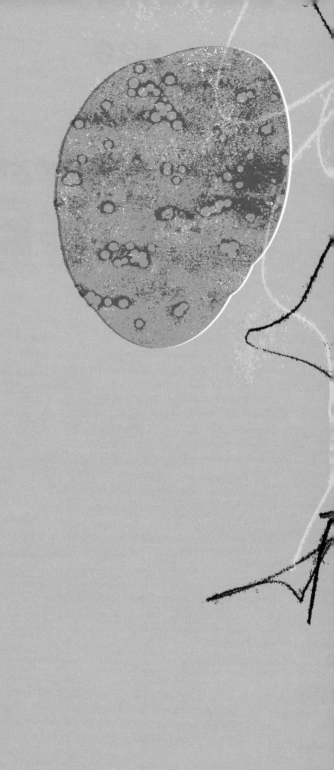

ITALIAN GREEN SAUCE

SALSA VERDE

Salsa Verde was one of the most popular sauces in the middle ages, and its popularity has stood the test of time. It is an essential accompaniment for zampone and Boiled Calf's Head (see pages 132-133). You can liven it up by adding a few finely chopped walnuts and a few basil leaves or simply play around with it by substituting other herbs of choice.

1 bunch (about 200g) flat-leaf parsley, stems discarded
2 cloves garlic
1 hard-boiled egg yolk, mashed
1 slice white bread, soaked in wine vinegar for
   20 minutes
200-250ml extra virgin olive oil
Sea salt and freshly ground black pepper

Put the parsley and peeled garlic cloves in a food processor. Process until very finely chopped.

Transfer to a mixing bowl and add the mashed yolk. Squeeze the soaked bread dry and add to the bowl. Mix together.

Slowly add the oil while stirring the mixture, as if you were making a mayonnaise. Add enough oil to have a creamy sauce. Season with salt and pepper, to taste, and refrigerate for about 1 hour before serving.

SAUCE GRIBICHE

Sauce Gribiche is a mayonnaise made with hard-boiled egg yolks instead of raw ones. It is usually flavoured with capers, cornichons and herbs and is traditionally served with poached calf's head.

3 hard-boiled eggs
Sea salt and freshly ground black pepper
1 tablespoon vinegar
100ml extra virgin olive oil
1 teaspoon Dijon mustard
1 teaspoon finely chopped chives
1 teaspoon finely chopped chervil
3 sprigs tarragon, leaves only, finely chopped
1 teaspoon capers
2 small cornichons, finely chopped

Mash the hard-boiled egg yolks in a mixing bowl. Pass through a fine sieve into a bowl. Season with salt and pepper. Stir in the vinegar and slowly add the olive oil, whisking all the while, as if you were making a mayonnaise.

Once the oil has been fully incorporated and you have an emulsion, add the chopped white of one egg, the mustard, herbs, capers and cornichons. Taste and adjust the seasoning, if necessary.

FRENCH PARSLEY SAUCE

SAUCE PERSIL

This sauce is a wonderful, subtle accompaniment for poached brains, calf's head, calf's feet or stuffed pig's trotters. If you are not in the mood for offal, you can also use it with poached fish. The choice of broth here will depend on what dish you are serving the sauce with – if I am serving this sauce with Stuffed Pig's Trotters (see page 44), I simply use the trotters' cooking liquid.

100ml broth
6-8 sprigs flat-leaf parsley, leaves only
100g unsalted butter
1 tablespoon flour
pinch cayenne pepper
¼ teaspoon lemon juice
Sea salt to taste

Put the broth in a small saucepan and bring to the boil. Remove from the heat and drop in most of the parsley (leave a little to chop finely and use as garnish). Leave to infuse away from the heat for 10 minutes. Strain.

Put a third of the butter in another saucepan and melt over a very low heat. Take off the heat and stir in the flour. Add 200ml boiling water, stirring all the time with a whisk, so as not to have any lumps.

Add the strained broth, the rest of the butter diced into small cubes, cayenne pepper, lemon juice and salt to taste. Stir in the chopped parsley and serve immediately in a pre-heated sauceboat. If you need to re-heat the sauce, do it in a bain-marie so that the butter does not become oily.

SERVES 4

BLANQUETTE SAUCE

SAUCE POUR LA BLANQUETTE

A classic sauce, often associated with veal cheeks. You can prepare it with baby onions as below, or without if time is tight. The sauce will be excellent either way.

14-16 baby onions (about 200g)
75g unsalted butter
1 tablespoon plain flour
450ml stock (see pages 110-111)
2 egg yolks
Juice of 1 lemon
100ml crème fraîche
Pinch grated nutmeg
Freshly ground white pepper
3-4 sprigs parsley, finely chopped

Peel the baby onions and put in a small pan with 25g of butter and 2 tablespoons of water. Cook, stirring regularly, over a low heat for 10-15 minutes or until they are done but not mushy. Cover with a clean kitchen towel and set aside.

Melt the rest of the butter in a saucepan over a low heat and stir in the flour. Gradually add the hot stock, stirring all the time with a whisk so as not to have lumps, and let bubble, stirring occasionally, for about 10 minutes. Take off the heat.

Whisk the egg yolks and lemon juice into the cream. Then slowly incorporate into the sauce to thicken it. Season with the nutmeg and pepper to taste. Taste and adjust the seasoning if necessary. Use with the lamb's cheeks in the Head Dinner For Two on pages 110-111.

SERVES 4

HERB BUTTER

BEURRE AUX HERBS

Adding knobs of this wonderful herb butter to the Lamb's Kidneys Baked Inside Potatoes on page 71 will make them even more luscious. This butter is also delicious with the liver or heart kebabs on pages 114-115, and it goes marvellously well with regular steak or meat brochettes.

200g unsalted butter, softened and diced into cubes
1 tablespoon strong mustard
4 sprigs flat-leaf parsley, finely chopped
8 sprigs chervil, finely chopped
6 leaves tarragon, finely chopped
Sea salt and freshly ground pepper, to taste

Put the butter in a bowl. Add the remaining ingredients and, with a fork, mash the butter to blend it with the herbs and mustard. Shape into a thick sausage. Wrap in aluminium foil and refrigerate until you are ready to serve it. You can also slice it and freeze it for later use.

VINAIGRETTE

Here is a basic vinaigrette which can be varied endlessly by adding different herbs; 1-2 tablespoons of chopped basil to use with a green bean salad for instance, the perfect accompaniment to Foie de Canard en Papillottes (see page 14), or 1-2 tablespoons of tarragon leaves to add extra flavour to boiled lamb's tongues (see pages 110-111). The variations are as long as the list of herbs available.

1 tablespoon Dijon mustard
$3/4$ tablespoon vinegar
3 tablespoons extra virgin olive oil
Sea salt and freshly ground pepper

Put the mustard and vinegar in a small mixing bowl. Add salt and pepper to taste and mix well together.

Stir in the oil slowly, as if you were making a mayonnaise, until you have a creamy vinaigrette – if you add the oil too quickly, the dressing will separate. Taste and adjust the seasoning. if necessary.

SAUCE RAVIGOTE

There is a wonderful restaurant in Paris, Chez Denise, where they serve Tête de Veau (the best ever) with Sauce Ravigote instead of Gribiche (see page 126). The meat is beautifully cooked – tender without being so cooked as to have lost all texture – and the taste is so clean that you wonder if you are really eating what was, not so long ago, a hairy and bloody head. Their ravigote is more like a vinaigrette with tarragon, whilst the following version is more like a béchamel with white wine and vinegar and herbs. At Chez Denise, the ravigote is served at room temperature, while this one needs to be served hot. I like both, although the vinaigrette-style ravigote is much quicker to prepare. Simply add tarragon leaves to the vinaigrette opposite and it becomes a ravigote.

50g unsalted butter
15g plain flour
300ml white stock
4 tablespoons tarragon vinegar
4 tablespoons white wine
25g shallots, very finely chopped
12g chives, finely chopped
5g chervil, finely chopped
5g tarragon, finely chopped
Sea salt and freshly ground black pepper

Make a béchamel sauce by melting 20g of butter in a saucepan over a medium heat. Stir in the flour and keep stirring for a couple of minutes. Add the stock and stir until completely smooth. Let simmer while you reduce the vinegar and wine.

Put the vinegar, wine and shallots in another saucepan. Place over a high heat and boil until reduced by two-thirds. Add the béchamel and simmer for 5 minutes. Take off the heat and add the remaining butter and herbs. Season with salt and pepper, to taste.

GLOSSARY

Blood

'This is a dish (blood soup) that 6-8 years old girls make themselves but which young boys also prize highly. When it is ready, some of the soup is poured into a flat dish and the boys lie on their stomachs round this and eat like dogs, while the small girls eat with their hands from the pot.'
Sverdrup on the children of Reindeer Chukchi, 1901

The mention of blood as food immediately conjures up images of blood-sucking vampires biting into the necks of nubile virgins. However, you don't need to be a vampire, real or imagined, to like animal blood.

Most cultures eat blood in one form or another and blood puddings (boudin) are made all over Europe. The filling for boudin is basically pig's blood and fat, although the Irish use sheep's blood for drisheen (their version of boudin). In France, they may add onions, chestnuts or small cubes of cooked head meats. In Spain they add rice and in Scotland oats. Whatever the mixture, it is seasoned with spices and herbs, funnelled into intestines and cooked very gently in a broth. In Iceland, where the women make a lot of blood sausages during the slaughtering season in the autumn, the sausages are pickled in whey-barrels.

Boudin is not the only edible blood product. In Spain, congealed blood is sold in blocks for people to use in different ways. The most common use is for it to be diced and sautéed with onions to serve as a tapa (encebollada in sangre). In Thailand, people add cubes of congealed blood to fish tripe soup. In France, they have Sanguette, a speciality from the Languedoc which was very common when chickens were killed at home. It is still prepared in some rural areas. The chicken is bled over a deep plate. Then the blood is seasoned with crushed garlic, chopped parsley and sometimes sautéed cubes of lean bacon and left to congeal before being fried in a little lard. The pan is deglazed with a little vinegar and the resulting sauce poured over the sanguette.

A very different version of sanguette is made in the Béarn. The Béarnais prepare theirs with the boiled cheeks, tripe and spleen of calf. These are diced and sautéed with cubes of congealed calf blood. When the meats have coloured, chopped onion, garlic and parsley are added. A little flour is sprinkled all over, some stock added and the whole dish is simmered for about half an hour. Towards the end of the cooking, sliced cornichons and capers are added.

The blood of hare, rabbit or chicken is also used to thicken sauces in civet dishes and others. Brazilian chicken in blood 'frango ao molho pardo' is similar to a chicken dish from the Nivernais called poulet en barboille, where the chicken is first cooked in red wine with bacon, baby onions and lots of garlic. When cooked, the sauce is thickened with the blood that was reserved for that purpose.

In Italy, pig's blood is used in a sweet preparation, sanguinaccio, which is found with some variations in Calabria (al cioccolato, when it is cooked with milk, sugar, cocoa powder, almonds and cinnamon, or con il riso, when it is prepared with rice, sugar, raisins, cinnamon and lemon zest). Sanguinaccio is also found in Campania (alla napoletana, where the blood is cooked with milk, chocolate, sugar and candied fruit). A version also exists in Sicily where it seems to have its roots in Arab cooking as I found the recipe in a book called La Cucina Siciliana di Derivazione Araba. The French also have a sweet boudin, from the Nord Pas-de-Calais region, boudin à la flamande which dates back to the late 18th century. The blood is seasoned with onions, salt, ginger, cloves, pepper, sugar and cinnamon, then finally raisins are added.

The Norwegians also use blood to make savoury cakes while the Japanese dry the blood of rattlesnakes to sell as an aphrodisiac.

Brains

> 'Have I lived to be carried in a basket like a barrow of butcher's Offal, and to be thrown in the Thames? Well, if I be served Such another trick, I'll have my brains ta'en out and buttered.'
> Shakespeare, The Merry Wives of Windsor III.v.4-6

Brains are probably the most delicate and finest of all offal, perhaps not so much for their taste as for their soft, creamy texture. Some people think that calf's brains are superior to lamb's but I find both just as good. Brains are very fragile and you need to take great care while preparing them. They need to be soaked, for about half an hour in several changes of cold water to rid them of any excess blood, then the thin outer skin is peeled – no easy task, though dipping the brains in water every now and then helps loosen it. They are then poached in a court bouillon for about 3 minutes to firm them up before using in one of several different ways, the simplest being dipped in seasoned flour and shallow-fried in butter.

Caul

> 'The fold of membrane loaded with fat, which covers more or less of the intestines in mammals; the great omentum.'

Caul as defined by the Webster's dictionary, a perfect description for a membrane that is often used to enclose fillings, meats, brochettes or different terrines. The purpose of using caul is dual, as an envelope but also, for its fat content, to help keep whatever is wrapped in it moist. You can buy caul fresh or salted. I prefer to use it fresh but if you can only find it salted, soak it for 10 minutes before using.

Cocks' combs

The best-known use for cocks' combs is in the classic financière sauce, the garnish for the classic vol-au-vent. I have never seen them sold in England but there is no reason why you cannot order them from an adventurous or knowledgeable butcher. The preparation is rather fiddly. They need soaking, blanching, then whitening, ie. cooking in a mixture of water, flour, lemon and salt for about 10 minutes to stop them from blackening. Then they need scraping with a small knife to get rid of the rough exterior. Once this is done, they are rinsed and rubbed with a little salt to get rid of the last rough bits. Cocks' combs are very rarely used nowadays and when they are, it is more for their gelatinous texture and shape than for their taste. The Russians also use cocks' combs to make a terrine where the diced combs are set in an aspic made with chicken stock, wine and lemon juice.

Ears

Most people balk at the idea of eating ears but I love the contrast between the crunchy cartilage and the gelatinous skin. The preparation is rather tiresome and some of it will bring you dangerously close to feeling that you are dealing with a human ear, ie. removing hair, scraping the wax, etc. As a result, I prefer to eat them in a restaurant or at friends' houses, but here is what you need to do if you want to prepare them yourself. First make sure your butcher cleans them really well before he gives them to you. Even then, you still need to scrape them, singe them, wash, blanch and wash them again to get rid of any scum. After this they are ready to be boiled, for about 2-3 hours with or without the rest of the head, and served as is with a sauce ravigote or gribiche, or breadcrumbed and fried in very hot oil.

Eyes

> 'For dessert there was simply a handful of bird and fish eyes picked out of the pot'
> Vibe, 1938

Eyes are probably the biggest taboo when talking about offal. Even Fergus Henderson at St John's has not served them yet. And, of course, there is the eternal cliché about Arabs and their predilection for sheep's eyes. Well, apparently it is not only them who are keen on the delicacy. The Russians view them as an aphrodisiac. This unsubstantiated piece of information was passed on to me by Mr. Guérin who was one of my offal butchers in Paris when I tested recipes there. He also said that they eat them stuffed (imagine the number of heads you need to produce a plateful of stuffed eyes). Well, perhaps they do and perhaps they don't but I have never tried them nor even seen them. However, I have often eaten sheep's eyes, whenever we had sheep's head, and yes, I did from when I was very young. They have a nice chewy texture without being tough, a little like that of squid but without the slipperiness. The secret is to remove the inky, black middle bit without bursting it before you bite into the gelatinous eye socket. I have also eaten fish eyes which are equally delicious but not those of whales, which the Japanese consider choice morsels. The Eskimos eat seal eyes and here is what Hoygaard wrote in 1941 of the Angmagssalik Eskimos: 'The central nervous system and the eyes are considered very good and usually fall to the lot of the hunter who has caught the animal.'

Feet

Feet are rich in gelatine and calf's feet are those normally used to thicken broth and give it body while pig's and lamb's are served in many different ways: in salads and sauces, or breadcrumbed and grilled or also in the case of pig's trotters, used as a casing to make stuffed feet.

One of the most famous French recipes for pig's feet is pieds de porc à la Ste Menehould. The feet are tightly wrapped in cheesecloth, to keep their shape, and cooked for at least 24 hours, and sometimes up to 40 hours, in a strongly flavoured broth until the bones are so tender that you can eat the whole thing. It is said that they were the undoing of Louis XIV who stopped in Ste Menehould on the road to Varennes to feast on one of his favourite dishes. The delay allowed the revolutionaries to catch up with the royal family and arrest them. I was not able to find a proper recipe for pieds de porcs à la Ste Menehould. All the good ones are jealously guarded by those who make them. The best thing I can do is to recommend trying them at Le Pied Rare, a simple café/restaurant in Paris, in the Bastille. The owners were given the recipe by the

inn-keeper they worked for in Ste Menehould and they regularly win prizes for their pieds de porc. You can also try them at the Soleil d'Or in Ste Menehould. They are quite unlike any other pig's trotters you will have ever tasted.

Another unusual way of preparing feet comes from Morocco, where they cook calf's feet in a sweet-spicy honey sauce. The result is astonishing and totally exquisite.

The Italians are also very keen on trotters and one of their best-known exports apart from pasta and Parmigiano is zampone, a kind of pig's feet sausage where the feet are boned and stuffed with ground pork meat and rind. Zampone, as well as cotechino (a sausage with the same filling but encased in pork skin) are traditionally served on New Year's Eve, with salsa verde and lentils. Both zampone and cotechino need long simmering, 3-4 hours, and have to be wrapped in cheesecloth to prevent them splitting and losing their shape during cooking.

Giblets

'...the burnished gold of the crusts, the fragrance exuded by the sugar and cinnamon, were but preludes to the delights released from the inside of the pie when the knife broke the crust. first came a soice-laden haze, then chicken livers, hard-boiled eggs, sliced ham, chicken and truffles in masses of piping hot, glistening macaroni, to which the meat juice gave an exquisite hue of suede.'
The Leopard, Giuseppe Tomasi di Lampedusa

Giblets include neck, liver, gizzard and heart in England but in France where they are known as abattis, they also include the head, feet and wings. The livers are sautéed, grilled or made into pâtés, the gizzards grilled or confit (cooked in fat) and the wings marinated and grilled. The head, neck and feet are used to impart flavour to sauces and stocks although they are perfectly edible and quite delicious.
The Chinese are very keen on chicken, goose or duck feet and prepare them in myriad ways. Another edible part from inside the chicken that few people know about is unhatched eggs. These can be left inside the

chicken to cook, sometimes forming an attractive necklace around the stuffing, or they can be carefully taken out and fried.

Alycot is a famous old-fashioned French stew made from giblets. The word is made up of three different ones: ale (aile/wing), y (et/and) cot (cou/neck). 'The days of gatchére, of chère-lie, when we sacrificed many subjects (geese, ducks, turkeys) we make, with the giblets, the gizzards and necks, an excellent starter that we call alicot.' (from Simin Palay, *The Cuisine of the Béarn*).

Heads

> 'After all there's a lot in that vegetarian fine
> flavour of things from the earth garlic of course
> it stinks after Italian organgrinders crisp of onions
> mushrooms truffles. Pain to the animal too.
> Pluck and draw fowl. Wretched brutes there at the
> cattlemarket waiting for the poleaxe to split their
> skulls open. Moo. Poor trembling calves. Meh.
> Staggering bob. Bubble and squeak. Butchers'
> buckets wobbly lights. Give us that brisket off
> the hook. Plup. Rawhead and bloody bones.
> Flayed glasseyed sheep hung from their haunches,
> sheepsnouts bloodypapered snivelling nosejam
> on sawdust. Top and lashers going out.
> Don't maul them pieces, young one.'
> James Joyce, *Ulysses*

Only lamb's heads are cooked and served on the bone. They are boiled, steamed, roasted or even smoked as they do them in Norway (smalahove). Calf's and pig's heads are boned and the meat (snout, ears, tongue and sometimes cheeks) is either cut up and sold separately or rolled like a roast and boiled to serve with a sauce ravigote or gribiche. Another way of preparing head meat is en fromage (head cheese or brawn) where the meats are cooked until tender, diced and left to set in their liquor. Of course, there are other ways of preparing head like in the following, extremely complicated recipe from Plumerey, published in his 1843 book *l'Art de la Cuisine au XIX siecle*, where he explains how to prepare *tête d'agneau à la Pascaline*:

'Take four sheep's heads; they should be perfectly skinned; bone them, and put them to soak, as well as the four brains and four tongues; take three lamb's livers that you will sauté with half the amount of fresh *lard*, fine herbs, salt, pepper and spices to make a stuffing, and twelve sheep's trotters that you will cook with the tongues; you will also cook the brains, but separately; when the tongues and brains are done, you will cut them in large cubes and, with mushrooms, you will make twelves croquettes; now take the blanched sheep's heads and fill them with the stuffing; tie them tightly; cover them with a few slices of lemon; cover them with pork fat and cook in a good casserole; have ready about twelve studded lamb's sweeetbreads; reserve the trimmings; have a sauce *tournée* in which you will have put two handfuls of mushrooms; you will reduce the sauce and thicken it with six egg yolks; then you will strain the four sheep's heads; untie them; arrange on a large round plate, the nose part on the outside; cut each trotter in two, put three in between each head; cover with the sauce, and arrange the twelve fried croquettes all around, the twelve sweetbreads piques and twelve bread crusts cut in the shape of crests; throw the mushrooms and sweetbread trimmings in the sauce and over the heads.'

Not a recipe you are going to rush to make but it gives you a good idea of how elaborately offal was prepared in those days.

A type of head that people do not often think of is fish head, a great delicacy in Singapore prepared in a curry sauce. The Asians are not the only ones to appreciate fish heads. The Scots were also very fond of them. I have found several recipes for dressed cod's and haddock heads filled with fish liver in *The Scots' Kitchen* by F. Marian McNeill. Here is a rather intriguing one for Crappit Heids, as stuffed heads are called, from the Isle of Lewis:

'Take half a dozen haddock heads and livers. Chop the livers, which must be perfectly fresh, mix them with an equal quantity of raw oatmeal, add pepper and salt, and bind with milk. Stuff the heads with this mixture, and boil them with the fish. The liquor makes good stock for fish soup. A similar stuffing is made with cods' livers, but the body, not the head, is stuffed, through the gullet.'

Hearts

It is sad that nowadays most English, or American people for that matter, consider hearts to be dog or cat food. They may not be the finest offal but they can be used in delicious preparations and have the added advantage of being very cheap. They can be stewed, stuffed and braised or grilled.

Intestines

'Fish intestines are cut up, cleaned, washed, boiled and eaten; boiled by themselves in water, not to be mixed with other (other parts of) fish or else with the head if the rest of the fish is dried; these intestines, fat, are the Lapps' delicacy...'
Drake, 1918

One of the most famous uses for intestines is in andouillettes, a fat French sausage made with pig's intestines that are either grilled or shallow fried and served with mustard. Andouille sounds similar but is quite different. It is made with intestines but in a very large sausage and is smoked for two months, hence the black skin. It is then tied, cooked in water or broth and dried. It is generally eaten cold, thinly sliced, but it can also be served hot after having been simmered in broth.

In Italy, intestines from milk-fed calf or lamb are used to make pajata, a Roman speciality, or brochettes. In Sicily the brochettes are grilled and sold on the streets – stigghiole is what you need to ask for if you want to try them. Similar versions of intestines brochettes exist with slight variations in Sardinia and Umbria. The South Americans have their own version which they call chinchulines while the Turks and Greeks wrap skewered lamb's lights with intestines and grill them to produce kokoreç or kokoretsi. The Lebanese fill intestines with rice, meat and chickpeas to cook alongside stuffed tripe and the Chinese cut them up to cook in a sauce and serve for dim sum. The English, Irish and Americans have their own chitterlings or chitlins, fried or grilled intestines, while the Eskimos eat fish intestines. These were also common food, in

northern Sweden where the intestines of sea trout were boiled and considered to be full of goodness. And, of course, pig's or ox intestines are also used as casings for all kinds of sausages.

Kidneys

'Mr Leopold Bloom ate with relish the inner organs of beasts and fowls. He liked thick giblet soup, nutty gizzards, a stuffed roast heart, liver slices fried with crustcrumbs, fried hencods' roes. Most of all he liked grilled mutton kidneys which gave to his palate a fine tang of faintly scented urine.'
James Joyce, *Ulysses*

The finest kidneys are those from calves although both lamb's and pig's kidneys are also very good. The latter need soaking to rid them of the strong smell and taste. You can buy kidneys with or without their protective fat. I generally ask my butcher to remove the fat and the core. Whale kidneys are also eaten straight after the catch, boiled in salted water.

Liver

'I am weary of whales. I have eaten whale boiled, fried and minced; the liver, heart, brains, and kidneys of young whale, and best of all, head fin boiled, cut in thin slices when cold, and eaten with thin slices of dry bread. It has a firm white substance and a pleasant nutty flavour.'
Elizabeth Taylor, 1890's

The smooth, buttery texture of liver, be it that of calf, duck, goose, monkfish or cod to name but a few is one of the ultimate delicacies. The finest of red livers is undoubtedly that of calf, although both lamb's and pig's are also excellent. Chicken livers are in a league of their own, softer in texture and totally delicious provided that, first, they come from an organic bird and, second, that they are not overcooked. In fact, except for pig's, no liver should be cooked beyond pink, otherwise the texture changes from melting to rubbery. Liver can also be smoked. In the Tarn, they marinate pig's liver in a highly seasoned marinade before tying it like a rôti and smoking it. The liver is thinly sliced, sautéed in oil and the pan deglazed with a little vinegar to provide a sauce. In Alsace, people mix chopped calf's liver with chopped onion, parsley and a little fine semolina to make big quenelles. The quenelles are poached in a white consommé and served with a beurre noisette.

The best-known of white livers is foie gras, either duck's or goose. I prefer duck's foie gras. The liver is smaller and somewhat less fatty. The Japanese have their own 'foie gras', that of monkfish (ankimo) although, technically, it is not really foie gras as the fish is not fattened artificially and the texture is closer to that of roe than liver. Ankimo is generally steamed and served cold with ponzu (the juice of citric fruit) and chopped spring onions. I found monkfish liver in the fish markets in Spain. You can buy it separately or attached to the head. I tried it a la plancha on the advice of the fishmonger and steamed à la japonaise. The latter was definitely the better way to prepare it. I also found canned cod's liver in Spain which was melting and delicious, and I assume healthy as it was preserved in its own oil.

Lungs

Lungs are mainly used in sausage making. They are my least favourite offal. They have a spongy texture and are very red when raw but turn a rather off-putting grey colour as soon as they start cooking.
The *Larousse Gastronomique* recommends beating the mou (lungs in French) to tenderise them.

Marrow

There are two kinds of marrow, bone marrow, from the shin of beef or calf and spinal marrow which is part of the nervous system and has a charming name in French: amourettes (little loves, a name that is also used for testicles). Bone marrow can be used in several different ways. It can be extracted and poached to serve on toast or on steak; or the bones can be roasted, a signature dish of Fergus Henderson at St John's restaurant in London.
The traditional way to make rissotto in Italy is by using bone marrow instead of, or together with butter or oil. Bone marrow is in fact pure fat and will melt if left long enough on the heat.

Spinal marrow is quite different, more like brain than marrow from the shin bone; and it doesn't melt when cooked for too long. Instead it hardens and turns rubbery. Before BSE, lamb's spinal marrow was a mainstay of the mezze menu in Lebanese restaurants. It was poached and dressed with olive oil and lemon juice. Both texture and taste are delicate but, because of BSE, you cannot get hold of it here any longer.

Palates

Palates were very popular in the past. There are several recipes for them, in the *Larousse Gastronomique*, in Hannah Glasse and in many other old cookbooks. They are no longer used today but if you were to find them, this is how to prepare them. Soak them first then boil until tender in a water and flour mixture so that they remain white. Once they are cooked, peel and serve with a sauce ravigote or gribiche. Sometimes you do get a piece of palate with tête de veau in French restaurants. More often than not, it is not peeled and has a most unpleasant gritty feel, a little like the skin of tongues.

Spleen

But I am pigeon-livered, and lack gall
To make oppression bitter, or ere this
I should have fatted all the region kites
With this slave's offal. Bloody, bawdy villain!
Remorseless, treacherous, lecherous, kindless villain!...
For murder, though it have no tongue, will speak
With most miraculous organ.
Shakespeare, *Hamlet* II.ii.554-558, 570-571

Spleen is not used widely except possibly in sausage making. However, there are countries where it is appreciated. The Sicilians have a spleen sandwich, *pani cu i meuza* or put more simply *milza*, which is sold on the street. The sliced spleen and other bits of offal like lungs, etc. are fried in animal fat in large metal pans and stuffed into buns with ricotta cheese. I can't say it is one of the most appetising sandwiches I have ever had but many Sicilians are very keen on them. This is not to say that I don't like spleen. In fact, one of my all-time favourite dishes is t'hal (a Lebanese spleen dish) where the spleen is stuffed with garlic and coriander and braised in vinegar. Gorgeous.

Sweetbreads

There are two types of calf's sweetbreads, the gangly ones that come from the throat and the round, nicely shaped ones, called *pomme de ris* in French, that come from around the heart. Sweetbreads are connected to the thymus gland and disappear as the animal grows older. Calf's sweetbreads are finer than those from sheep. Depending on how bloody they are when you buy them, you may need to soak them first, until they become white. Then poach and press down (only calf's) to flatten them. After this they are ready to be prepared in all kinds of different ways, simply dipped in flour and fried, braised, grilled, baked, cooked in pastry, etc. Sometimes calf's sweetbreads are spiked with cubes of fat, truffles, tongue or ham.

Tail

There are two kinds of tails, the bony ones from the ox and pig that have rich meat on them or the fatty ones from the fat-tail sheep that have no bone and are highly valued in the Arab world. Oxtails and pig's tails are cooked in stews, while the fat from the fat-tail sheep is eaten raw, diced very small, with raw liver or used in cooking instead of butter or ghee to impart a rich, special flavour to stews and other dishes. Oxtail and pig's tails need long, slow cooking until the rich, juicy meat falls off the bone.

Testicles (Fries)

Testicles are a part of the fifth quarter that most people reject outright, simply because of what they are. If they only knew how delicious the taste is and what a delicate, melting texture testicles have, they wouldn't be so hasty in their rejection. Testicles need to be peeled before cooking but the butcher will generally do that for you. There is no need for any special preparation and by far the best way to cook them is to dip them in seasoned flour and gently fry them in butter until golden, adding a squeeze of lemon juice just before they are ready. It is very important not to overcook them as they will lose their velvety texture

and become hard and rubbery.

In France, testicles are poached before frying but I don't think this is necessary. In Iceland, ram's testicles are preserved in sour whey, while in Japan, whale testicles are boiled and served with a vinegar sauce. I prefer lamb's testicles to those of bull but there isn't that much in it except for the size. I haven't tried cock's or capon's testicles, known as rognons blancs (white kidneys) in France, but they are also highly prized.

Because of the sexual connotation, testicles are almost always referred to by a different name except in the Arab world where they are simply called balls of sheep. The Italians call them gioielli (jewels) or animelle, while the French alternate between les joyeuses (the happy ones, in the feminine, and I guess one can understand why), animelles or amourettes (darling ones or little loves, confirming the opinion that the French know how to live). Amourettes is also the name given to spinal marrow. The Americans, puritanical as ever, refer to them as prairie or mountain oysters, also as Montana tendergroins, cowboy caviar, swinging beef, and calf fires, (the latter two showing a less puritanical streak). Calf's testicles are reputed to be a favourite of president George W. Bush, and were apparently a staple on the menu when he was governor in Texas.

Tongues

Tongues, ox or calf's, are sold either fresh or cured. Lamb's tongues are only used fresh as are ducks' and goose, the latter two being great favourites of the Chinese. If used fresh, ox, calf's and lamb's tongues need to be soaked then boiled to rid them of the blood and then peeled. Ducks' tongues have a funny little bone inside them and those of geese need some preparation before they are ready for use. Whale tongues were also appreciated. There are several references to whale tongues being eaten in the middle ages, amongst them an account by the French surgeon, Ambroise Paré (1517-90), describing a whaling expedition off the Atlantic coast of France. Two bundles of whale tongues were then presented to King Charles IX and his mother Catherine de Medici

– Paré describes the tongue as tender and delicious.

Tripe

Till cramm'd and gorg'd, nigh burst With suckt and glutted offal.
Milton, *Paradise Lost* X. 633

Ox tripe has four distinct sections, the four stomachs: honeycomb (bonnet in French), reed tripe (caillette), bible tripe (feuillet) and thick seam (panse). Honeycomb and thick seam are usually sold pre-cooked, often bleached. It's best to avoid bleached tripe as much of the flavour and texture will have disappeared in the process. Reed and bible tripe are hardly ever pre-cooked and need thorough cleaning before cooking. In fact, all tripe unless pre-cooked needs lengthy washing before use. The four types are needed for making tripes à la mode de Caen, one of the most famous French tripe dishes, otherwise honeycomb or thick seam will do. Another famous French tripe dish is the tablier de sapeur, a speciality from Lyon, where large squares of cooked thick seam tripe are marinated in white wine, lemon juice and mustard, then dipped in egg and breadcrumbs and fried.

Pig's and lamb's stomachs are obviously much smaller than calf's or ox and do not have the reed or bible section. The tripe itself is a lot thinner and more suitable for filling. William the conqueror loved tripe cooked in the juice of Neustrie apples and Rabelais' Grargantua was conceived after his mother, Gargamelle, had eaten a large plate of gaudebillaux, the tripe of coireaux beef (fattened from when they were born on their mothers' milk or in fields where the grass grew twice a year).

Another kind of tripe that many people are unaware of is fish tripe. Salted cod's tripe is a great delicacy in Barcelona while other dried fish tripe is used in Thailand and in China to make soup.

Udder

'Boil sow's udders and cut into pieces. Add some pike meat which has previously been ground in a mortar, minced chicken, raw eggs and oil. Mix together and season with pepper. Moisten with garum and wine and add a few raisins. Cook in an earthenware pot and once done, transfer the stuffing to which you will have added becfigues (a little bird found in abundance in the south of France, also known as béguinette), peppercorns and pine nuts to another pot that has already been lined with pastry. Cover the filling with a layer of pastry and bake in the oven.'
Apicius

There are two places I know of where you can try udder. One is Jame' el Fna in Marrakesh, the world-famous square with its ambulant cook-stalls, set up every evening as the sun sets. The cooks are grouped by speciality with an offal corner where the vendors sell boiled sheep's heads and other offal including udder. The other place is a café/restaurant in Madrid that specialises in frying offal off-cuts, if there is such a thing. There I had a mixed fry-up of the glands that line the intestines (moist and tasty), udder (dry and bland), spleen (so-so) and even trachial tubes (pleasantly crunchy). The fat in the huge frying pans was rendered from the lining of the stomach, intestines, heart and other bits. This all-out offal meal has been my most extreme offal experience to date. I would not go so far as to say that it was exquisite but it was certainly memorable, both for me and for my Spanish friend, Alicia Rios, a wonderful food performance artist who found the place for me and took me there. We are both intrepid eaters but after the meal, we knew we would not be rushing back to that place. The Madrilenos, on the other hand, seemed to be sold on it. The place was heaving when we ate there.

SELECTED BIBLIOGRAPHY

Académie des Gastronomes, Académie Culinaire de France *Cuisine Française,* Le Bélier, 1971

Ali Bab *Gastronomie Pratique,* Flammarion, 1950

Allen, Darina *Irish Traditional Cooking,* Gill & Macmillan, Dublin, 1995

Allen, Jana & Gin, Margaret *Offal, Gourmet Cookery from Head to Tail,* Pitman Publishing, 1976

Sonia Allison and Myrna Robins *South African Cape Malay Cooking,* Absolute Press 1997

Andrade, Margarette de *Brazilian Cookery, Traditional and Modern,* Charles E. Tuttle, 1965

Benoît, Félix & Clos-Jouve, Henry *La Cuisine Lyonnaise,* Solar, 1980

Bifrons *La Cuisine Française,* Edition de Cap, 1965

Boni, Ada *Les Cuisines Regionales d'Italie,* Editions Planète, 1970

La Cucina Romana, Edizioni della Rivista 'Preziosa'

Boulay, David *East of Paris,* Ecco, 2003

Brissaud, D. & Péchinot, J-L *Un Festin de Cochon,* Editions du Chêne, 1998

Carnacina, Luigi *Great Italian Cooking,* Abradale Press, 1968

Chaudieu, Georges *Boucher, Qui Est-Tu? Où Vas-Tu,* Éditions Peyronnet, 1965

Chen, Pearl Kong, Chen, Tien Chi & Tseng, Rose Y.L. *Everything You Want to Know about Chinese Cooking,* Barron's, 1983

Andrews, Colman *Catalan Cuisine,* Grub Street, 1997

Curnonsky *Bons Plats, Bons Vins,* Maurice Ponsot, 1950

Davidson, Alan *The Oxford Companion to Food,* Oxford University Press, 1999

North Atlantic Seafood, Perennial Library, 1989

Dunlop, Fuschia *Sichuan Cookery,* Michael Joseph, 2001

Eidlitz, Kerstin *Food and Emergency Food in the Circumpolar Area,* The University of Uppsala, Sweden, 1969

Febrés, Xavier *Menuts i Altres Delícies Porques,* Edicions El Mèdol, 1998

Fitzgibbon, Theodora *A Taste of Scotland,* Avenel Books, 1970

Floyd, Keith *Floyd's Food,* Absolute Press 1981

Fosså, Ove *A Whale of a Dish: Whalemeat as Food,* Oxford Symposium, 1994

Gisladdóttir, Hallgeröur *The Use of Whey in Icelandic households, from Milk and Milk Products: from Medieval to Modern Times,* proceedings of the Ninth International Conference on Ethnological Food Research, Ireland 1992, ed. by Patricia Lysaght, Canongate Academic, Edinburgh 1994

Gault-Millau *Les Trois Cuisines de France, Gibiers Abats,* Deux Coqs d'Or

Good Housekeeping *100 Recipes for Unrationed Meat Dishes,* Good Housekeeping Magazine

Gossetti della Salda, Anna *Le Ricette Regionali Italiane,* Casa Editrice 'Solares', 1967

Gouffé, Jules *Le Livre de Cuisine,* Librairie de L. Hachette et Co., Paris, 1867

Gray, Patience *Honey from a Weed,* Prospect Books, 1997

Hayat, Dinia *La Cuisine Marocaine de Rabat, Un Art et une Tradition,* Ribat el Fath, 1990

Hartley, Dorothy *Food in England,* MacDonald, London, 1954

Heath, Ambrose *Meat,* The Cookery Book Club, 1971

Heller, Christine A. & Scott, Edward M. *The Alaska Dietary Survey, 1956-1961,* US Department of Health, Education and Welfare, 1967

Hyman, Philip & Mary, ed *L'Inventaire du Patrimoine Culinaire de la France:* Provence-Alpes-Côte d'Azur, Midi-Pyrénées, Corse

Jack, Florence B. *Ninety Nine Ways of Cooking U.C.P. Tripe and Cowheel,* United Cattle Products, Manchester

Jung-Feng, Chiang & Schrecker. Ellen *Mrs. Chiang's Szechwan Cookbook,* Harper & Row, 1976

Larousse Gastronomique, Montrouge, 1937 to 1938

Lucarotti, Rolli *Recipes from Corsica,* Prospect Books, 2004

Mason, Laura & Brown, Catherine *Traditional Foods of Britain,* Prospect Books, 1999

McNeill, F. Marian *The Scot's Kitchen with Old-Time Recipes,* Blackie & Son Limited, 1929

Montagné, Prosper & Salles, Prosper *Le Grand Livre de la Cuisine,* Ernest Flammarion 1929

Mark, Willie, ed *Cooking with Honk Kong Top Chefs,* The Affairs Publishing Co. Ltd, 1985

Nasu, Keizo *Considerations on Whale Culture,* in Shoku-no-kagaku (Dietary Science), p. 84-96, 1986

Oliver, Raymond *La Cuisine,* Bordas, 1967

Olney, Richard, chief consultant *Offal,* Time-Life Books, 1981

Ohnishi, Mutsuko *Mrs Ohnishi's Whale Cuisine,* Kodansha, 1995

Patten, Marguerite, O.B.E. *The Victory Cookbook,* Hamlyn, 1995

Pudlowski, Gilles *Les Trésors Gourmands de la France,* La Renaissance de Livre, 1997

Pueyo, Victor Manuel Sarobe *La Cocina Popular Navarra,* Caja de Ahorros de Navarra, Pamplona, 1995

Rayes, Georges N. *L'Art Culinaire Libanais Real Pub Food,* Absolute Press, 2001, ed. by Meg Avent

Rivera, Guadaloupe & Colle, Marie-Pierre *Frieda's Fiestas, Recipes and Reminiscences of Life with Frida Kahlo,* Pavilion Books Limited, 1994

Rorlien Saue, Solfrid *Norwegian Cooking, Det Norske Samlaget,* Oslo, 1988

Rose, Mademoiselle *100 Façons d'Accomoder le Veau,* Flammarion

Schwabe, Calvin W. *Unmentionable Cuisine,* University Press of Virginia, 1979

Serrahima, Joan *Manual Moderno de Chacineria Casera,* Editorial de Vecchi, S.A. Barcelona, 1986

Sexton, Regina *'I'd ate it like chocolate!': The Disappearing Offal Food Traditions of Cork City,* Oxford Symposium, 1994

Siesby, Birgit *Blood is Food,* PPC 4, Feb 1980

Teubner, Christian *L'Encyclopedie du gout,* GaultMillau, 2002

Thompson, David *Thai Food,* Pavilion Books Limited, 2002

Toulouse-Lautrec & Joyant M. *La Cuisine,* Agence Internationale d'Edition, 1966

Trang, Corinne *Essentials of Asian Cuisine, fundamentals & favorite recipes,* Simon & Schuster, 2003

Useros, Carmina *El Toro en Los Fogones de Albacete y su Provincia,* Carmina Useros, Tinte 24, Albacete, 1992

Valby, Jean *Gastronomie,* Edition de la Revue Bonne Table et Tourisme, 1989

Verroust, J., Pastoureau, M & Buren, R. *Le Cochon, Histoire, Symbolique et Cuisine,* Editioms Sang de la Terre, 1987

White, Florence, ed. *Good Things in England,* The Cookery Book Club with Jonathan Cape Ltd., 1968

CONVERSION TABLE

Do keep to either metric or imperial measures throughout the whole recipe. Mixing the two can lead to all kinds of problems.

25g	1 oz	200g	7 oz	375g	13 oz	15ml	1 tbsp
50g	2 oz	225g	8 oz	400g	14 oz	150ml	$1/4$ pint
75g	3 oz	250g	9 oz	425g	15 oz	300ml	$1/2$ pint
100g	4 oz	275g	10 oz	450g	16 oz (1lb)	450ml	$3/4$ pint
150g	5 oz	300g	11 oz	1kg	2 lb	600ml	1 pint
175g	6 oz	350g	12 oz	5ml	1 tsp	1.2l	2 pints

INDEX

ACKNOWLEDGEMENTS

I am always astonished at how generous friends and colleagues are with their time, knowledge and contacts during the research of a book. I am also always astonished, and rather annoyed at myself, at how consistent I am at forgetting to mention a few. And I would like, from the start, to apologise to those whom I have excluded and thank them together with the following:

In England

Gillian Riley for finding me recipes in old Spanish and Italian cookery books. Liz Seeber for suggesting useful books and finding them for me. Fuschia Dunlop for sending me Chinese recipes. My brother, Joseph Helou and his wife, Isabelle for introducing me to their Brazilian friends, Maria Graca Fish at the Brazilian Embassy and Claudia Shakardjian who all provided me with information on Brazilian offal. Angela and David Barlow for lending me a book on Norwegian cooking. Arabella Boxer for letting me use some of her recipes. Leila Sansour for sending me offal recipes from Russia. Jane Levi for being such a sweet friend and a great recipe tester. Catherine Brown for sending me her recipe for Crappit Heads. Paul Hughes and everyone at the Ginger Pig, for general advice, Everyone at Blagden's fishmongers for advice on fish offal. Peregrine and Patricia Pollen for their brilliant editorial advice, Anna Mcnamee, Don & Yoko Brown, Helen and Nasir Saberi Miriam Polunin, Susie Burgin, Elisabeth Luard, Jeremy Lee, Caroline Davidson and her father, the late Alan Davidson. And, of course, Jon Croft, my charming publisher and editor, who had the idea for a book on offal at the same time as I was thinking of writing one. Also at Absolute Press, Meg Avent, and Matt Inwood for his brilliant design and Andy Pedler for his lovely art work. And last but not least, Leigh Goodman for doing such a wonderful job promoting the book.

In Greece

Diane Kochilas for introducing me to Aristides Pasparakis who made me my first kokoretsi and garthoumbes in his idyllic native village, Anogea in Crete, which we then ate in his cousin's charming cafe in the main square.

In France

Anne Marie and Guy de Rougemont for being such wonderful friends, lending me their lovely flat in Paris and having me to stay in their beautiful house in the Camargue so that I could test recipes. I am also grateful to them for taking me to wonderful restaurants to taste various offal dishes even if one of the meals ended in disaster when I fell into a ditch and emerged with all my crisp white linen caked with mud, not to mention my bloodied face. Jacqueline de Guithaut, another wonderful friend who always finds me useful information and recipes on whatever subject I am researching. Amina Al-Sabah for lending me her stunning flat in Paris to test even more recipes. Mr. Guérin, boucher/tripier in the 14th, who took the time to talk to me about various offal and gave me excellent recipes as well as showed me how to bone a calf's head. Philip and Mary Hyman for their help and guidance and also for letting me stay in their flat to use their fantastically well-equipped kitchen and their marvellous library of cookery books. Seth Rosenbaum for finding me literary quotes about offal. Also Jose Alvarez; Jean Lafont, Fabio Montrasi and Alex Toledano.

In Spain

My lovely friend Alicia Rios, food performance artist extraordinaire, for kindly putting me up in Madrid and taking me to wild places where we ate bits of offal that I had never tasted before; also for her help in recommending excellent books on Spanish food as well as finding me a place to stay in Barcelona. Luisa Ortines who made me feel at home in her airy flat in Barcelona and her friend Yamandu for taking me around the Boqueria and translating for me. Leopoldo

Rodés Castañé for taking me to some of the best restaurants in Barcelona and outside to taste amazing offal dishes. Señora Maria Font Llupia for giving me fabulous recipes and her gorgeous sons Josep Maria and Xavier in Mercat Sant Antoni for providing me with first class pig's offal and charcuterie. Isidre and his wife at Can Isidre in Barcelona who gave me one of the best ever recipes for tripe. Also Santi Santamaria at Fabes and the great chefs at Can Matteu and Quo Vadis. The late Donald Munson who was such a marvellous and fun shopping, cooking and eating companion. Margaret and Colin Visser for introducing me to Mercat Sant Antoni and letting me test the kidneys in sherry recipe in their kitchen. And Bernadette O'Shea who came to visit in Barcelona and proved to be a willing tasting companion, daringly tucking into some pretty unusual dishes.

In Italy
Armando Manni, for arranging a delicious offal dinner at Il Convivio, one of the best restaurants in Rome where the supremely talented Chef, Angelo Troiani, prepared a truly refined offal tasting menu. Ilaria and Franco Buitoni and Suni Agnelli, all wonderful friends and hosts, having me to stay at their different houses whenever I visit Italy and always being there to help with whatever I need help with.

In Morocco
Mortada Shami, owner of the fabulous Stylia restaurant in Marrakesh, for arranging amazing offal dinners so that I could taste the different specialities of the country. El Nguir Hajj Mostapha in Marrakesh who has his own meshoui stall by Jame' el-Fna where they bake the most delicious sheep's heads not to mention whole lambs. Also the various butchers in the weekly markets outside Marrakesh for taking the time to talk about offal and answer my questions.

In Norway
Ove Fossa for sending me an impressive amount of information on offal in Norway, the Faero Islands, Iceland and other nordic countries,

In Lebanon
My mother, Laurice Helou, for giving me all the Lebanese recipes and being a tremendous support, always.

In America
Charles Perry for finding me Turkish recipes during his last visit there. The late Catherine Brandel, and Peter Fuhrman for transcribing the Thai fish tripe soup recipe and always being there with good advice when I need it.

In Tailand
My great friend, Vippy Rangsit, her sweet daughter Bey and her wonderful cook, Tiew. Tiew initially made the fish tripe soup in Thailand and had Peter transcribe the recipe. But then she came to London with fish tripe that Vippy had given her for me and, with Bey translating, I was able to watch her make it and of course taste it. Perfectly exquisite.